# CHOPPING ONIONS

**Fred Horgan**

**Designed and produced by:**
Ken Spink, Inspiration Graphics,
61 Union Street, Saint John, New Brunswick E2L 1A2.

Printed and bound in Canada.

First Edition November 2002.


National Library of Canada Catologuing in Publication

Horgan, Fred, 1942-
    Chopping Onions/Fred Horgan

ISBN 0-9731852-0-1


    1. Horgan, Fred, 1942-.  2. Saint John (N.B.)--Biography.  I. Title.


LA2325.H72A3 2002            971.5'32            C2002-904901-6

Front cover illustration by Kimberly Horgan.
Market Slip.
Acrylics on canvas.

*"Chopping onions
...doing something, anything,
reminds you of someone,
and you smile although nobody's there"*

Alden Nowlan

For Barb, who prodded me for years
to write something, so I did.

# Table of Contents

# Acknowledgements & Foreword

In a recent e-mail, my friend Roger Ploude, Chairman of the Department of English at the University of New Brunswick, hit the nail on the head. "Don't lose sight of the glory in the commonplace", he encouraged. Perhaps to this thought should also be added the advisability of occasionally seeking out what is commonplace in the glorious.

These essays take a shot at both themes. Some seek out the "glorious" in what otherwise might pass as insignificant: people I've known, events I've experienced, places I've visited. Others parse very complicated human emotions in search of an elusive universal, the commonality that gives them meaning.

I have many people to thank for their support and encouragement: the editorial staff at the Saint John Telegraph Journal, formerly the Times-Globe, especially Rob Linke and Ron Barry; Fred Cogswell, for permitting the use of his poem "Like Two Slant Trees" and for providing helpful criticism on short notice; Robert Gibbs, for granting permission to use the Alden Nowlan allusion in the title; Terry Comeau, a friend and former colleague at Saint Malachy's High; Jim Hope for a photo of Sunset Lake and Brian Lynch for a photo of his dad, Gerry; my brother Jim for taking the time to proof-read each and every essay; my daughter Kimberly for permitting the reproduction of her painting which appears on the front cover.

Most of all, I want to thank my most severe critic yet most enthusiastic supporter, my wife Barb, for never giving up on her belief that "there's a book in there somewhere". In a very real way, we wrote this together.

Fred Horgan
September, 2002

# "Like two slant trees they grew together"

...Fred Cogswell

It was a beauty: a 3-speed, orangy-red Raleigh with handbrakes, chain guard (back then, you usually had to buy one separately) and an airpump that snapped neatly onto the frame under the seat. For better than three months I'd admired it at the back of Pascal-Emerson's sports department as it sat smugly among the CCM's and balloon-tired no-names, a vastly superior bicycle if ever there were one.

It was a grading present (grade 7 or 8, I think) from my mother and father, with a matching light and horn from my great-aunt Elizabeth. When they arrived that afternoon, the light and horn were still boxed so I got to attach them to the handle bars. Both were battery operated, and the horn had a little button activator that attached thumb-high, just beyond the handgrip.

I remember riding madly, horn buzzing, from Exmouth to the big hill on Cliff Street just to see if I could climb it sitting down. After all, this was no ordinary machine; that miracle of engineering, first gear, was unconditionally guaranteed to eliminate huffing and puffing. The lower half of the hill presented no problem, but I had to work a zigzag pattern for the final thirty or forty feet to avoid lifting bum. Even then, the two or three guys who came with me for the test run were really impressed.

For the next few years, that bike and my fishing rod were my most prized possessions. With the help of a couple of pieces of string the rod fitted perfectly under the crossbar, leaving plenty of room to hang my wicker creel in front of the handlebars.

Every evening I'd leave our summer place on Dolan's Lake and peddle up the road to the brook that ran beside the old mill. Then I'd hide the Raleigh in the bushes, slap on some insect repellent, and hit the half dozen or so pools hidden in the thick alders.

This was my own private spot. No-one else ever fished there; at least I can't remember meeting anyone. Within an hour at the most I could always count on fifteen or twenty decent-sized brookies, plenty for a late snack or early breakfast. Then back on my bike and home again, riding as hard as my legs would allow, peddling with all my might, subconsciously converting contentment into animation. Afterwards I'd sleep like a baby.

It was that way when we got our first rowboat too. It was a twelve foot, wooden flatbottom with the usual middle and stern seats and a small, triangular spot at the bow. We kept it at the edge of the lake just below the camp, moored to a big boulder that sat a few feet from shore. By the time we got it (I was eleven or twelve then), the Raleigh had seen its day, so the boat and I would venture regularly to the far side of the lake to fish the deeper pools that couldn't be reached from the heavy shoreline. It was a beautiful spot, maybe eight feet deep, with water so clear you could see every movement on the silt bottom. As it got dark, whatever breeze there was seemed to die off and the lake became a mirror so clear you could count the stars on its face. I'd keep an eye on our camp on the side of the mountain until its shape melted into the darkness. That's when I'd head home, rowing as furiously as I could, finally reaching shore spent but satisfied. Then I'd sleep.

The year after I started teaching I bought my first new car. It was a beige Barracuda with bucket seats, stick shift, tachometer, and an enormous rear window that took the better part of a month to clean. The progression was complete: Raleigh to rowboat to Barracuda. Life was good. When things were going particularly well for me, the `Cuda and I would head for some back road and kick up some dust until we were both tired. Then home again, a football game, feet up, and I was out of it.

I guess that's another idiosyncrasy attached to being young. Through childhood, adolescence and early adulthood we tend to lean heavily on *things* when we feel the need for an escape or emotional release.

But patterns are made to be broken.

In January of 1967, after an especially boring badminton game at the Saint Peter's Rec Center, I met an old friend at the back of the Riviera on Charlotte Street. Neither of us had much to do so we ended up back at his place for a casual card game with his sister and a young lady who boarded with them. It was all quite innocent at first, just a way to finish an otherwise uneventful evening, but after fifteen or twenty minutes I found myself increasingly fascinated by the young lady. She had an engaging laugh and a sense of humour to match, and was certainly easy to look at.

The following evening we went bowling and then for a drive. Conversation flowed freely, really quite a rarity for me on a first date, and by the time I took her home I had this inexplicable urge to find a dark road and drive like the dickens.

I found an appropriately dark road without any problem, and it was completely deserted so there was no one around to bother me. But for some reason I couldn't understand, my foot was light on the gas peddle. In fact, I didn't really feel like driving: fast or otherwise. Instead, I parked the car and just sat there.

I'd had this feeling once before. It was near the end of my third year of university, just after I'd decided that I wanted to enter the seminary. We were having a campus retreat that week and I'd made an appointment with Father Andy Reid, a visiting Augustinian, to see if there was anything special I should be doing in the way of preparation during my final undergraduate year. When I arrived at the room that served as his temporary office, he ushered me in with a hearty "great to have you with us", sat me down, and suggested we get started with my telling him a bit about myself.

This was perfectly logical to me so I took a seat and

started to talk. I'm really not sure what I said or how long I took to say it, but I clearly remember what happened next: I simply stopped talking. I have no idea how long I was silent, but I do remember one thing as clearly as if it happened only yesterday: I knew with absolute certainty that the priesthood wasn't the place for me. It wasn't like Saul on the road to Damascus either: no blinding epiphany or peal of thunder; just the unequivocal certainty that there was something else I was meant to do. Father Andy must have sensed it too. He rose to his feet, walked across the room with extended hand, then led me to the door.

"Great to have had you for a while, anyway".

When I left, I went for as long and very leisurely walk, savouring the tremendous peace I was feeling.

Now, I'm not a great believer in things paranormal or extra-sensory so I won't try to share in any greater detail the experience I had that evening in Father Andy Reid's little office. I will add this footnote though. Only once since have I experienced the same awareness: that night, just me and my `Cuda, on the side of a pitch-dark road in the country. At that moment I knew with unexplainable but complete certainty that some-

thing important was happening or about to happen. How, or when, or why, I couldn't say; but it was happening none the less. For only the second time in my life I instinctively knew it was time to slow down.

That young lady and I have shared better than three decades. We've raised four great kids, an assortment of cats, a beagle, two hamsters and a dozen or so goldfish on the side. Oh sure, I still have a car and even a bike, but they aren't as important to me as they used to be.

I now understand that the only way to get somewhere important is slowly, and that truly precious things in life have meaning only when they're shared with someone you love.

Fred Cogswell's poem *"Like Two Slant Trees"* says it best:

*"Lean on me", he said*
*loving her weakness*

*And she leaned hard*
*adoring his strength*

*Like two slant trees*
*they grew together*

*their roots the wrong way*
*for standing alone.*

*Chopping Onions*

# *"He Who Destroys A Good Book Kills Reason Itself"*

...John Milton

One Christmas when I was in late grade school I received a copy of "Hans Brinker And The Silver Skates" from my cousin, Rita. I've no doubt it was her mother who made the actual choice since Rita and I were roughly the same age and had yet to appreciate the power of the written word.

I remember being relatively unimpressed the afternoon Uncle Charlie dropped it off at the house. After all, anyone with half a brain could tell by the wrapping it was a book, and I'd far rather have received something I could play with, preferably insanely expensive with moving parts. So it was that from Christmas morning until Tuesday or Wednesday of the week after New Year's, it sat unopened beside my mother's soaps and Dad's newest batch of socks, in the darker shadows below the lower limbs.

It was a particularly brutal Christmas season that year. We didn't get a lot of snow but it got really cold, cold enough to keep the space heater in the living room fired up continuously. There wasn't much a kid could do outside without risking his nostrils freezing shut so my brother Jim and I were forced to improvise indoors. This didn't work out very well either; most of the time we ended up fighting over whatever it was both of us urgently required but neither of us really wanted.

That's when I picked up the book from Rita, opened the wrapping, and casually broused the front cover. It had a picture of this kid in a funny looking costume skating his heart out on what looked like a canal or something. Curiosity led me to page one; I started to read, and two hours later when Mom called me to supper I was still reading. After supper I was back at it again (to the total delight of my parents) and by bedtime I was half finished, a task I wrapped up the next morning, literally (no pun intended) curled up in a big chair by the front window. I was hooked.

Great-Aunt Elizabeth was living with us then and it was she who suggested I walk up to the library and see if I could find something else I liked. I walked, I found, I read, and I've been reading ever since. After that, for most of my junior and senior high years, Saturday was curl up day and that chair was my magic carpet.

There was a problem though. When I was in school, most of the stuff we read, voluntarily or otherwise, had been written by people who'd long ago turned their toes to the daisies. I used to think that in order to be a decent writer you had to be almost (and preferably totally) dead! More than that, I could count on one hand the number of Canadian authors I'd been exposed to and still have a couple of fingers left over. I never argued this, but it always struck me as quite odd that other than Roberts, Carman, and a short story or two by Morley Callaghan, Canadians hadn't a lot to brag about in the literary world.

So it was that I embarked a couple of decades ago on a personal crusade to prove myself wrong. What a discovery it was: Laurence and Atwood; Layton, Birney, and Klein; Richler and Cohen. The more I read, the more I was haunted by the old adage, "Show me your literature and I'll tell you your history." Here it was, magically unfolding before me... not the United States or Great Britain but Canada, a unique mosaic that defied description.

My greatest pleasures were the discoveries close to home: that Northrup Frye was raised and educated in Moncton; that P. K. Page lived for a while in Rothesay; that one hundred and twenty-five years ago a Saint John girl, May Agnes Flemming, was making a small fortune writing serialized novels for Boston Magazines. That a gentleman I'd encountered dozens of time at dances at the Armories, Dan Ross, was also the most prolific author in the world!

I was so impressed that I approached our Principal of the day and sought permission to offer Canadian Literature 120 at our school. I envisioned a course that would not only promote an appreciation of good literature but would also dispel any notion that to be a successful writer one first had to be a dead foreigner. I wanted the young people to read, and in doing so to realize that writers, unlike our legendary salmon, don't turn belly up immediately after spawning. Why not, I reasoned, expose students not only to reading but also to those who wrote.

In the years that followed, through classroom visitations, we came to meet some of the finest authors New Brunswick has to offer: Fred Cogswell, David Adams Richards, Robert Gibbs, Kay Smith, William and Nancy Bauer, Kent Tompson, and many others who through their own generosity graced us with their readings, experience and wisdom. I wouldn't presume to speak for the young people, but for me personally literature had become as real as my own neighbourhood. "Curling up" was as easy as a walk around the block.

Sadly though, those literary neighbourhoods, yours and mine, are changing. Casual little chats that used to take place over a backyard hedge are now committed to e-mail. Anyone with access to the internet can call up a Shakespearean play, any of thousands of newspapers and magazines and probably before long most of the literature presently housed in the largest libraries in the world. The day is fast approaching when the pure joy of a walk to the library or local bookstore to browse with kindred spirits will be gone forever. In a few decades time (or less, I suspect) what will be the availability of books and magazines? Will the printed word be a luxury reserved for the affluent? Ironic, isn't it, that the 'in' term used to describe comfort with a computer is "literate".

What will happen to that classic metaphor for contentment, "curling up with a good book"? Will there be good books to curl up with, or will the option be to curl up with a laptop and surf the literary net?

A few weeks ago I caught a familiar yet infamous image on The Learning Channel. It was of a crowd of frenetic soldiers and citizens tossing books onto a communal pyre, gleefully destroying the written word. Anyone who appreciates history will realize that this act has been replayed countless times, and in each instance has come to stand for warped priorities, for societies that have (in the interest of 'progress') lost touch with things truly beautiful and valuable.

It strikes me as very sad that our generation, high tech as it is, has put a new twist on the old art of book-burning.

# The Memorable Week Letter-Writing Came To Saint Malachy's

Though I taught high school English for thirty years, I've never considered myself a man of letters, at least not in the sense of a Thoreau or Steele. True, my vocation necessitated that I read a fair amount and it helped that I loved to talk literature, but if truth be told I identified more with Robert Gibbs appraisal of Fred Cogswell: "more a lover of poets than poetry".

I do love to write though. It's more cathartic than creative. There's nothing so purging as punching one's soul into a keyboard confessional and waiting for the penance. Maybe I write for the same reason people sail oceans and dogs chase cars: a satisfaction more in the act than the product.

Except of course for that time with the Free Press
Weekly.

When I was still in high school my summers were spent
in Lower Golden Grove. Usually there was no problem in finding something to do, but every now and then the pace would
slow down a notch and it was adventure time. That was the case
one Saturday afternoon in late August of 1959. The fish weren't
biting and an August fog had rolled inland from the bay just
enough to chill us into putting on a jacket. Jim Hope and I were
sitting on the veranda of the summer camp leafing through a
copy of the Free Press Weekly, a Winnipeg publication I'd bor-
rowed from Smith Cathline, our mailman. The middle pages
formed a double spread called the "Pathfinders", a kind of teen
forum on just about anything. Subjects ran from kissing on the
first date ("teen sex" hadn't been invented yet) to what was right
or wrong with television or the relative merits of the Edsel and
the SuperSport. Penpals were freely solicited.

This wasn't my first exposure to Pathfinders. A year or
so before, on a day much like this one, I'd come across a simple note from a girl in Red Deer looking for a penpal her age
who lived in the east. I took a chance, dropped her a line, and
our literary friendship lasted for two or three years. In one of
her letters she mentioned she'd received "hundreds" of responses to her original letter, some from as far away as South
America.

All this was running through my mind as Jim chuckled
aloud over a scathing attack on country music in general and
Johnny Cash in particular. It had been penned (badly) by a
music major (or so he said) from somewhere in Ontario.

"Can you believe something that bad could ever get
published? I guess they'll take anything. What would they do if
they ever got a good letter; really good!"

Jim slapped the paper with his left hand as if to punc-
tuate the "good" and the "really".

Both idea bulbs went on simultaneously.

A little rummaging in the drawer under the telephone yielded a clean sheet of paper, at least clean enough for a rough draft. Then back to the veranda, pencil in hand, ready and waiting for the muse to arrive.

Nothing.

"Any idea what to write about?" Jim was on the top step facing the lake.

"Not a clue. You?"

"Nothing. Let's take a look at the kind of thing everyone else writes about."

He opened the paper once again and scanned the letters for that week. "Nothing very inspiring. The best one's that trash about Cash." He was chuckling over his unintentional rhyme when it hit me.

"Just a minute. If he can get all that mileage out of an attack, why can't we get the same from a defence!"

We had it: "A Defence of Johnny Cash!".

With the help of my good friends Mr. Roget and Mr. Webster, we were under way; three drafts and an hour or so later it was finished, a showcase of polysyllabic gymnastics that started with nothing and went nowhere but sounded great along the way. Then a rewrite in my best printing (we didn't want to risk anyone's missing a word), a lick and a stamp, and it was ready for mailing.

A few weeks passed without any reply whatsoever. Every morning we'd check the Free Press with increasing frustration. Not a thing. I'd put down my city place for the return address, so every day we'd call Johnny MacFadyen, the guy who ran the store across the street from us on Exmouth and who collected our mail in the summer, to see if anything had arrived. It hadn't.

When September finally came around, it was back to the city and school for my grade 12 year at Saint Malachy's. For the first few weeks or so I'd call Jim regularly to see if he'd heard anything (he checked the Free Press every week), but after a while we more or less wrote it off as a bad bet and forgot about it.

October dissolved uneventfully. Dances were under way at the CYO and preparations for Hallowe'en were rolling along. Our first set of exams arrived in early November and by the time Remembrance Day was over we were already thinking about Christmas. The last thing on my mind was Johnny Cash and the Free Press Weekly, so I had to stop and think the evening Jim called.

"It's there!"

"What's there?"

"The letter. Pathfinders! It's the letter of the week! Covers about a quarter of a page!"

"You're kidding! Does it say anything else? About how great it is or anything? Any editor's note or something like that?"

"Nope. Just 'Letter Of The Week' across the top, and the stuff you wrote, with a black line all around it. It's two columns wide though!"

"Did they print the part about writing back to us, the address and all?"

"Yeh, it's all there. Maybe we'll get a letter or two! Who knows."

We decided we'd let a week or so pass before looking for any mail. It didn't strike us that by the time we'd received the paper it would've been read a week ago by everyone west of Toronto.

The next day I followed my usual habit of dropping into Johnny's store on my way home at noon hour. He fascinated me with his stories of the First World War, the things that had happened to him and the places he'd seen. He never made them gory or anything but I could always sense a profound seriousness in even the most harmless stories. I was to learn later he'd lost a lung to chlorine gas.

He was a man of habit. Most of the day he'd spend sitting alone in a big chair at the back of the store. Then when a customer came in he'd shuffle to the front counter and take care of him or her in a gruff rasp a lot of people mistook for disrespect. He rarely smiled and I don't think I ever heard him laugh.

I mention all this so you'll understand how surprised I was to find him standing at the front, elbows on the counter top, when I came in.

"How's she goin', John? Break your chair or something?" No answer. Just a stony stare.

Five seconds of ackward silence.

"What's the trouble, John? Pipes freeze up again?"

This was a private joke we had to excuse a bad mood for whatever reason. "Pipes freeze up again?" Then, "Stick a blow torch in your mouth for a few minutes. That ought'a take care of it!" This time it didn't seem to be working though. He just stood there, leaning forward on the counter, chin in his hands. I was getting a little uncomfortable.

Then he spoke. "Get any mail lately?"

In the confusion of the moment I didn't make the connection.

"Mail? Some. Why? What's the problem?"

He straightened to his full five foot, nine inches and reached for something on the floor. That's just about the time it struck me: Pathfinders! From behind the counter he lifted a mailbag the size of a potato sack and dropped it dramatically in front of me.

"Well you got some now!"

"Jim?"
"Yeh?"
"They're here!"
Pause
"Who's here?"
"Not `who'! `What'!"
"Okay then. `What's' here?"
"The letters! From Pathfinders! Three hundred and fifty of them!"

"How many you say?"

"Honest. Three hundred and fifty something. From everywhere! British Columbia, Saskatchewan, Manitoba, even some from the States. And there's one from California too. A whole bag of `em! Some of them smell real good too! I'm gonna open those ones last. And there's this one from Brandon with..."

"You gonna give me some, aren't you? How can I get them? Maybe you can send them over to the school somehow."

Jim was at Simonds when it used to be on Bayside Drive and I was at Saint Malachy's. I can't remember just how I got them to him, maybe through my Uncle Noel who taught there, but I do know I packed up fifty or sixty and sent them along. At this point in our marvellous adventure we had every intention of answering each one; Jim would take a bunch and I'd take the rest. That night alone I managed to pen about thirty or forty short responses. Then the magnitude of our problem began to strike home: three hundred and fifty pieces of notepaper times three hundred and fifty envelopes times three hundred and fifty stamps, at maybe ten minutes per letter. This would take forever, even if I could afford it.

What happened the next day made the decision really easy.

Noon hour. Johnny's store. Cold stare.

"How's she goin', John? Break your chair again? Pipes freeze?"

"Got any mail lately?"

Two bags this time. And two more after that. Even then they kept trickling in by tens and twenties! I took them to school by the hundreds and pawned them off on anyone who'd take five. I had no trouble getting rid of the smelly ones but the aromatic neutrals stuck like glue. What's worse, my locker started to smell like a perfume store, which wasn't too great in an all-boys school! Before long I ran out of people to give them to. The guys would duck into washrooms or out side doors when they saw me coming. I was persona non grata... in my own school! And

I still had a pile of envelopes the size of a termite mound in the corner of my bedroom.

There was only one way out that I could see. The furnace: the big one in the basement of the school where all the paper trash went on Tuesdays and Fridays. Every evening for the next week or two I packed three or four Dominion Store bags with letters. Then I'd get to school good and early, well before eight o'clock (school started at nine) and leave a closed bag at the bottom of each of the half dozen garbage barrels around the building. My mother and father were very impressed with my sudden obsession for getting to school early. Efforts like that had to pay dividends with higher marks, they reasoned. I didn't argue.

By January the letters had all but stopped. Jim and I both wrote to a favourite five or six for a while longer but eventually we closed the book on them too.

All this was a long time ago. A year later I was at Saint Francis Xavier University and Jim was in the Air Force. I was headed for the priesthood and Jim was going to be a pilot. Thirty-something years have slid by much faster than I'd have hoped. Today, we're both retired, me from teaching and Jim from NBTel. But I guess we still have a bit of the kid in us yet. Every now and then when we meet somewhere, he'll make a noise like a fighter jet while I bless him.

*Chopping Onions*

*Chopping Onions*

# *"O, What A Tangled Web We Weave, When First We Practice To Deceive"*

...Sir Walter Scott

Years ago we had a pair of cats named Salt and Fluffy. I'd like to say they answered to those names but I can't; near as I can remember they answered to nothing but the sound of a can opener.

They could be quite friendly when they wanted to be but still they were typical cats, using basement corners to dispatch occasional tokens of defiance. Salt led the way. We could always tell a little package had been deposited just by watching Fluffy sniffing around behind the furnace or under the workbench. Usually Salt got like this whenever we switched cat food or mislaid the little stuffed mouse he'd otherwise take out his frustrations on. That's when he'd stroll toward the back stairs, tail indignantly high, ready, willing and able to assert his singularity one more time. Fluffy, always the follower, would join the protest but her objection usually amounted to a claw sharpening excursion on an arm of the nearest available chair.

Later on, when Alf the Beagle joined our clan, the saga continued. Problem was, Alf had to stay home by himself most of the day, an alienation he didn't take to very kindly. His turf on fine days was limited by a twenty foot tether anchored to one leg of a picnic table on the back lawn. By the time we'd arrive home around five or so, he'd have excavated anywhere from a dozen to fifteen holes, each seven or eight inches deep. Before long our lawn started to look like a gopher farm. That's when we realized that Alf, like any other animal, was in dire need of his own space, so we found him a great home on a farm and, to the best of my knowledge, he's been eminently happy ever since.

Then there were the three or four hamsters whose names escape me at the moment. We kept them in a relatively large cage from which they regularly escaped, insubordinations that inevitably precipitated furious searches aimed at finding them before Spook, our cat of the day, could beat us to it. The plan didn't always work though. Spook, as harmless an animal as ever cornered a hamster, took it as his personal responsibility to fetch the errant critter and return it to us. Gingerly he'd lift the truant, kitten-like, by the nape of the neck, come looking for us and deposit his offering at our feet. One memorable morning we even woke up to find cat and hamster both waiting patiently at the foot of the bed!

The point is, we all need our space: cat, dog, hamster, or whatever. Call it wander-lust if you want, but sitting down for long periods of time has an unnatural quality to it. At least that's the way it's always been with me. Even when I was a little kid I was forever climbing fences, swinging from ropes or running somewhere. Usually it didn't get me into any trouble though, except for that one time in grade one.

I can't remember a thing about the walk to school on my first morning. I know my mother escorted me and I have no trouble imagining the route we took, but up until the nightmarish moment just before she exited the classroom, everything's quite blank. From that point on though, it's crystal clear: Mom slowly working her way toward the door as Miss Leahey skillfully distracted us with flowery little name tags she'd pulled from a paper bag on her desk. Those were the days when all teachers had to take at least one course in Skillful Distraction just to survive. Anyway, I caught on to the ruse when, eager to show off my flowery new name tag, I turned in the direction where Mom had been standing only to find a blank wall.

Panic! Gross stress!! If I'd been in a bed, I'd have wet it!!! And I wasn't alone. It was your classic group animal: everyone reacting in unison to the simultaneous awareness that we'd been abandoned, possibly forever. A nanosecond of silence sat heavy on the lot of us; then, from somewhere near the back of the room, the slight but unmistakable whimper of one child's mounting desperation. The flood gates opened. Miss Leahey, scarred veteran of the pedagogical wars that she was, wisely chose to let wailing dogs wail for a minute or so. Then, when the howling had subsided to little more than ineffectual blubbering, she carried on with whatever it was that was next on her agenda and life continued to unfold with inexorable objectivity.

For most of us the catharsis worked. Grade one was here, there wasn't a thing we could do about it, so it was time to get serious. In all fairness, Miss Leahey made it a lot easier for this to happen. She was a really nice person who seemed to care for every one of us. Maybe in the privacy of her stream of consciousness she had her personal favourites but if so she never gave us a hint of who they were. If we were good we were all favoured, and if we dared rub against the grade-one grain we were each reproved with equal severity.

After a week or two we were starting to pull together. Sure, there were the red birds and the blue birds and feathered metaphors of other colourations for each reading group, but most of the guys adjusted quite nicely.

Except for me. I missed having my space. I resented a world not of my choosing, dictated by bells and patrolled by adults other than my own parents.

Then came the day in late September when I rebelled. I guess it wasn't a rebellion really because it wasn't as if I'd meditated on it for a day or two beforehand. It's just like it was there so I did it!

It was a brilliant autumn afternoon and I was on my way back after the noon hour. As I passed the CYO I was distracted by city workers digging a hole of some kind so I stopped to watch. By the time I remembered where it was I'd been going, it was too late. Except for a few pigeons scavenging for sandwich parts, the school yard was deserted. What a beautiful day for a walk!

I don't remember feeling particularly guilty about the whole thing. It was as if someone had mistakenly left my cage door open and the temptation was too much to resist. Back towards Waterloo Street I went, letting my imagination wander through the garden of possibilities that were mine to reap: a walk uptown? climbing the roof of the old garage behind the Murphy yard? throwing a ball against a backyard wall? No, I don't remember feeling particularly guilty, not at first at least, but by the time I'd reached the Cathedral the enormity of my sin was starting to hit me. Call it the old Guardian Angel thing if you want, but I had this sudden picture of Miss Leahey and my mother, tears of humiliation flooding from my mother's eyes as Miss Leahey expressed her total disappointment in me.

Now I WAS beginning to panic! The entire six years of my life (or at least the three and a half I could remember) flashed by my eyes. The only thing I was certain of was that I had to sit down and figure this thing out, so I did, right there on the bottom step of the Cathedral. Clearly I had to find a place to hide, some place fairly close to home. That way I could stay concealed until school was out.

Eureka! I had the perfect spot: under the steps that led to the back door of the tenement where we lived. It was ideal: dry, sheltered from any possible squall and only thirty seconds from home. And as far as that sin thing went, I could always work it out with God on Sunday. My personal experience was that He seemed to be a pretty good guy, though Monsignor Cronin, His number one at the Cathedral, could throw a decent scare into you when he wanted to.

At that moment though it wasn't Monsignor Cronin or even God who had me worried; it was the wrath of mother. After all she'd been a teacher for quite a few years before my brother and I arrived on the scene and she took this "school" thing really seriously. Yep, Mom was my immediate concern.

With considerable stealth (as considerable as possible considering how loudly my knees were knocking) I made my way from telephone pole to telephone pole, pausing behind each one just long enough to make sure I wasn't being watched. Down one alley and up the next, dodging the three or four mongrels I didn't trust, I finally made it to the darkened grotto that would be my refuge for the next couple of hours and sat myself down.

Time passed far too slowly and before fifteen or twenty minutes had passed I was starting to get sleepy. The next thing I knew, Sport, the friendly spaniel who lived across the yard, was licking my face and making whining sounds. No doubt I had unwittingly invaded his territory and he was just finding a nice way to let me know. A quick glance at my Mickey Mouse told me it was a few minutes after three and time to crawl out of there and play out the rest of the charade.

Unfortunately though, the charade ended far sooner than I might have anticipated. No sooner had I extricated myself when I got the shock of my life. From somewhere above me and to my left a voice descended.

"Well rested, young man?"

I looked up, fully expecting to come face to face with God himself (or at the very least Monsignor Cronin) only to find my mother sitting three steps above me, looking, I might add, a lot sterner than usual.

"Sleep well?", she asked redundantly. And then, "How was school today?" It was more an undeniable indictment than a question. I'd be dead by nightfall.

I didn't die that night. I suffered a bit but I didn't die. No, it wasn't anything physical like a slap or three in the posterior region. Instead I wasn't allowed to trade comics for a week, had to be in bed by 7:30 each evening, and the most painful punishment of all: having to convince my parents all over again that I was old enough to be trusted. That was the hardest part: I'd betrayed the most sacred of trusts: that between parent and child. Even at six years of age I was perceptive enough to realize I must never do it again.

I'm proud to say that I remained faithful to the promise I made to myself and my mother that fateful afternoon. I've no doubt slipped a few times since then but never intentionally. I'd learned the best of lessons in the hardest of ways: there's no greater pleasure than a parent's pride, and no greater pain than a parent's disappointment.

# *A Christmas Secret*

As far as Christmas is concerned, I've always been a believer.

At first I accepted without question the image of the jolly fat man in a red jump suit flitting from roof to roof every Christmas Eve. After all, wasn't it on the radio that the air force or Prime Minister or someone really important like that had picked him up on a radar blip somewhere over the North Pole? And hadn't he been heading south, toward Canada? And didn't those gifts magically appear every Christmas morning?

I remember one special Christmas Eve I was standing at the front window straining my ears to pick up sleigh bells when I actually SAW him. Admittedly it was only a glimpse, more a blur really, but there he was, gracefully skipping from star to star with the assurance of a seasoned aviator. I ran to the kitchen where my mother and father were sitting so they could see him too but by the time we'd returned to the window he was gone.

"But he was there! Right over there!" I pointed in the direction of a half moon over Waterloo Street. "Right there! Honest!"

No, they didn't ruin it by telling me it was my imagination or anything like that; they fully understood what had happened. It was the essence of childhood: I believed and so I saw, and for the next hour or so I luxuriated in reliving every delicious detail as they listened patiently.

By the time I'd reached grade two or three, Christmas had moved beyond the jolly fat man story but was no less exciting. Every December my Great Aunt Elizabeth would give me five dollars to spend on my parents and my brother Jim, and I always managed to squeeze out enough for her too. I was beginning to appreciate the joy of giving. Mind you it's nice to receive, but there's nothing like having your own secret place to hide a loved one's Christmas tickle. I used to milk it for all the suspense I could get.

"Bet you can't guess what I got ya'."
"A book?"
"Nope."
"Toy?"
"Nope."
"Does it wiggle or make a noise?"
"No way."

And so on and so on, until the guesser got tired of guessing and grabbed a couple of Christmas mints. It was one of those special games where we both won.

By the time I'd entered high school I was up to my ears in the adolescent dilemma: too old to be a child and too young to be a kid again. Those were two or three Christmases that weren't much fun. By the end of November I knew everything coming my way because brother Jim and I would have sniffed out all the hiding places and rummaged through the loot. What made it worse, Christmas exams really cut into my shopping time and put a serious strain on my "joy of giving". If I were really lucky the holiday season might last forty-eight hours, only to disappear with leftovers on Boxing Day.

Those were confusing Christmases. It wasn't that I'd stopped believing; quite to the contrary. I was at the pompous age when believing was the opposite of understanding, and it would be a few years yet before I would understand the difference between faith and knowledge. My college years weren't much better. Christmas wasn't much more than a trip home, with ribbons and some pretty paper thrown in for good measure. I think the problem was I'd become so distracted by academics that I'd forgotten for a while the rapture of anticipation.

Then in 1964 I came home to stay. For the first time in four years I got the chance to enjoy firsthand the intimacy of a New Brunswick autumn, and with it returned the anticipation I had been missing. I was seven or eight all over again. The first snow, buying presents, finding the perfect tree, midnight mass: the magic returned with a warmth I hadn't felt for nearly a decade. I was a kid again, only this time I was wise enough to realize it.

When Kimberly, our first daughter, came along (followed by her sister Cheryl two years later), believing was suddenly very easy because they did most of it for me. *Their* excitement was *my* excitement; their faith, my faith. More than any other time of the year Christmas was for family, framed by traditions I hadn't even realized I'd inherited.

Then came the Christmas Eve my life completed another of its many circles. Our family had spent the evening watching "Miracle On Thirty-Fourth Street": not that new-fangled, artificially-coloured one but the original, in predictably glorious black-and-white (and on a black-and-white T.V., I might add). Anyway it was getting near the end, the part when the little girl discovers Santa's walking stick in the house of her dreams. Even when I was little it had always been a very moving scene and on more than one occasion I'd faked a trip to the bathroom before anyone had a chance to see how wet my eyes were. This time I avoided the problem by listening to the dialogue but not looking at the screen. Instead I watched our daughters curled up on the floor in front of me.

What I saw in their faces that night catapulted me back two decades to a different floor in a different home, to my brother and me in almost the identical pose watching the same Maureen O'Hara and Natalie Wood. At that moment I understood. The child believes what he or she is led to believe, and consequently the same child sees what he or she believes to be there. Unfettered by the myopia of adulthood, the child can part skepticism's veil and see whatever he or she wants to see, be it Santa, angels or the face of God.

I know more than a few adults will dismiss this as little more than verbal slight of hand but you don't have to take my word for it. Test it for yourself. This Christmas, rent one of those great old classics. It doesn't have to be "Miracle On Thirty-Fourth Street", though it works just fine. It could be any of the great ones that have stood time's test, like Jimmy Stewart's "It's A Wonderful Life" or Alstair Simm's "A Christmas Carol".

Here's the secret. Watch it with a child: faces really close, cheek to cheek even. Pay attention though. You have to be ready or you might miss it: those precious few seconds when the veil parts. Don't dare to blink; hold on really tight, and if you're lucky you'll live again an age when you too were young enough to come face to face with ... .

But that's something you'll have to find out for yourself.

# *A Letter To Santa, Christmas 2000*

Dear Santa:

My name is Freddy Horgan and I live in Saint John, New Brunswick and I'm fifty-eight years old. I've been a reasonably good boy this past twelve months (well, most of it anyway) and I'm sending this note so you won't have to worry about what to bring this Christmas.

You'll notice, Santa, that I really don't want anything for myself. Honestly, I'm not conning you in the hope of finding a new Grand Marquis under the tree. It's just that I've come to realize that watching others receive is much more satisfying (and lasting too). So for the past few weeks I've given some thought to what really special thing would make a lot of people happy. It may take a while for them to realize it, but that's how genuine contentment works. Instant happiness is about as satisfying as instant coffee and gets cold even quicker. No, what I have in mind is something that will challenge you and maybe require a little extra effort, but I know if anyone can do it, it's you, Santa.

To be honest, I was afraid for the longest while I wouldn't be able to decide on that special something. Perfect gifts aren't so easy, as I'm sure you of all people can appreciate. Then, a week or two ago, I had occasion to go uptown (here where I live, you have to be at least forty to know where "uptown" is). It was a December Saturday afternoon and I was parked in front of Market Square by the big wooden clock, looking up King Street. This is the part of Saint John, at least old Saint John, I've always associated with Christmas, the one I knew when I was growing up: colour and commotion, cars bumper to bumper, and thousands of people scurrying from store to store checking out Christmas bargains. This particular Saturday, though, one could have driven eight reindeer side by side up King without inconveniencing a soul. It was then I knew what my special gift, had I the power to order one, would be.

Santa, could you possibly arrange for all the malls to shut down for a few days and all those merchants to come back uptown? One weekend would do it. I'm thinking about the area around Union, Charlotte, and King. And do you think you could wave a wand or something and bring back Calp's and MRA's with their big window displays like in those old Christmas movies? Take all of us back to a time when walking and maybe a city bus were the ways people got around, when uptown was a December adventure, when toy displays at Woolworth's and Pascal-Emerson and Zellar's made a believer out of you whether you wanted it or not, when presents were carried in the bottom of a paper bag rather than the trunk of a car.

While you're at it, load King's Square with more Christmas trees than the city will ever need (*real* trees, not those artificially-scented, plastic ones), firs and pines that sell for two or three dollars and smell like only Christmas can smell. Make them so tightly packed that shoppers have to squeeze by one another to cross the Square, just like it used to be. To make things extra perfect, have Christmas movies playing at the Paramount, Strand and Capital, and lots of hot chocolate at the Riviera, Diana's, and Louie Green's. For a quieter moment, people could drop into Driscoll's Drug Store on Union, with its little booths along the back wall and the greatest peanut butter sandwiches west of home. There should be Christmas music in every store of course, but not loud and blaring: just enough to set the mood and get people humming. And lights; don't forget the lights! Lots of them in every colour imaginable, blinking a welcome six blocks wide.

For just a little while, take us back to a time when stores really did have basements to keep bargains in, when we had to go outside to get from one merchant to another, and when policemen in long coats blew whistles and stopped traffic to let us get to the other side of the street. Put a Salvation Army pot on every second corner and maybe a band or two wherever you can squeeze them in. And snow, and carollers, and candy-canes for a penny each.

Santa, I'm not so naive as to think we could leave it this way forever but a weekend wouldn't hurt, would it? It'll be just as busy and hectic as it is today but the genuine excitement of an uptown Christmas will make up for it all.

Thanks for reading my letter and say hello to Mrs. Claus and the reindeer for me.

Your friend,
Freddy

*Chopping Onions*

# *"Know when to fold"*

...Kenny Rogers

*"The Gambler"*

Blame my grandmother Lynch if you want. She's the one who introduced me to my first deck of cards when I was only three or four. She probably reckoned it a harmless enough diversion for keeping me out of mischief and dark corners while she and my mother exchanged the latest gossip. For hours at a time the two of them would sip tea and munch home-made cookies while I sat contentedly in the middle of the kitchen floor, creating tipsy little houses in every shape imaginable.

I got pretty good at it after a while. Before long I could exhaust an entire deck and start on a second one before an ill-timed opening of a door or window sent them scurrying like leaves in an autumn gust.

By the time I entered grade school I'd moved on to Crazy Eights, Go Fish and even a few rudimentary card tricks capable of dazzling anyone under the age of five who hadn't seen them before. I could shuffle medium well and deal with the best of them, so my father, a card freak himself, decided it was time to move up to a more challenging test: solitaire. One rainy Saturday afternoon he sat me down, ran me through a few hands and left me with the caution that I shouldn't expect to win every time I played. What he didn't count on was that I'd win the first one and from that time on I was addicted.

The itch is still there fifty years later. Twice a year a few of us get together for an evening of poker (the harmless variety where mortgaging one's belongings isn't necessary). And every month for a quarter century my wife and I joined three other couples, all close friends, for an exercise in frustration we liked to call Bridge. For the better part of an evening we'd rant and rave, absentmindedly trumping our partner's ace while simultaneously reserving a few moments to solve most of the problems plaguing humankind (and creating a few more to fill the void). Then we'd sit down to an always delightful meal, stretch, yawn and shuffle home to bed, enormously contented.

I get a charge out of any game that involves a full deck but for a long time my favourite was cribbage. There was a time when I could last an entire evening and never lose my concentration. Three or four of us would make it a point of entering at least one cribbage tournament a week, sometimes more. In those days there were plenty of places to choose from: a half dozen Legions, The Fish And Game Society at the Lily Lake pavilion, an occasional fund raiser in one church hall or another.

I even had a collection of cribbage boards in every material imaginable: plastic (in the nifty shape of a "29"), wood, even a metal one with aluminium pegs. They sat ceremoniously on a living room shelf at my parents' place (I was still single then), waiting patiently for someone, anyone, capable of counting as high as thirty-one to drop by. Most of the time it wasn't a terribly long wait.

Not long after I started teaching, Joe Breen and a few other teachers at school talked me into taking out a golf membership at Riverside. Joe was as consistent with clubs and irons as he'd been with hockey stick or baseball bat, which made him a great partner for a neophyte like me. As often as I could I'd join Joe and one or two others for a hundred or so swings and whatever advice he could give me without chuckling. I didn't get a heck of a lot better but I did get to wear outrageously-coloured golf slacks salvaged from discarded flags of the world.

Then came the day the big announcement was posted in the pro shop: a golf and cribbage tournament in two-person teams, each pair to play nine holes of golf and then ten games of cribbage. The lowest combined totals would pick up a few dozen golf balls, or new putters or the like. Well, I'd be the first to admit that golf was well down on my list of advertisable strengths, but cribbage ...now THERE was somewhere I could shine.

So it was that Joe and I pooled our respective talents and signed on. Of one thing we were certain: if Joe could just shoot his usual golf game and I could pick up a few "twenty-four" hands, we'd be unbeatable. And as an added bonus, he was no slouch at moving the pegs along himself. No question; it was ours for the taking.

The big afternoon turned out cloudy and cold, which meant nothing to me because my golf game was at least consistent: pathetic no matter what the weather. Joe would have preferred a warmer few hours but there was nothing we could do to change things so away we went. What happened next neither of us could have foreseen: I actually started hitting the ball! Mind you, length off the tee had never been a difficulty for me; no, direction was the root of my ineptitude. Two hundred and fifty yards? No problem, just so long as it didn't have to be a STRAIGHT two-fifty. But this day was amazing! Every shot straight as Pinocchio's proboscis at a fibbing bee. Joe too! Long and straight every time. We were nothing short of phenomenal. When the dust cleared nine holes later we were fifteen strokes under par (mind you, my handicap of twenty-something didn't hurt either).

Now for our real strength: the cribbage board. When we sat down for our first hand our confidence bordered on arrogance and, I fear, it probably showed. Hubris was rearing its ugly head. I was supremely certain this would be that "piece of cake" I'd always heard others talk about but had yet to experience for myself.

But too soon I came to realize the wisdom of the adage, "The mills of the Gods grind slow but exceedingly fine". Ten games later we were ashes. Not one win ...not a one! What's worse, we'd been skunked at least a half dozen times. The pain was excruciating, and no use looking for a little sympathy anywhere! "Tough luck, guys. Better stick to golf and leave the brainy games to someone who doesn't teach."

Late that night, cocooned securely in bathrobe and slippers in front of the television, I took a few moments to try to make some sense of it all. What went wrong! Was it the hand when I tossed two fives into the other guys' kitty thinking it was ours? Or maybe the one when I decided pegging was more important than keeping a good hand and got the screws put to me royally.

That's when I picked up the top two cards of a nearby deck and gently leaned one against the other. Then two more, and two more, and two more. Hey, this was a lot more fun than trying to pommel someone with a cribbage peg. My little castle grew to a bigger one, and then bigger still. Now this is REAL fun, I told myself.

"Told you so", whispered my grandmother over my shoulder from somewhere in the distance.

# *Father Carl*

When we were in high school, there was never a problem with where to go on weekends. Sundays, of course, were set aside for church, homework and the NFL, but Friday and Saturday nights were soundly booked. Matter of fact, there wasn't enough time to take in everything.

The big attractions were called the "Hi-Y"'s. Starting around eight or eight-thirty each evening, they were a safe meeting place for hundreds of regulars to dance and socialize for two or three hours of harmless fun.

On Fridays, we had a choice to make: Saint Peter's Recreation Center or the Assumption Hall. Most of the time it came down to simple geography: the gang from the west side would head for the Assumption, and the rest of us in the North, South and East would flock to Saint Peter's. Saint Peter's was my personal preference because either way I'd have to take a bus and the Assumption was at least another fifteen minutes away.

On Saturday, though, there was no hesitation. From 8:30 until 11 or 11:30, the CYO was where you'd find me. I guess part of the affinity was loyalty to the Cathedral parish where I'd served mass ever since I was old enough to say "Dominus vobiscum", but it was more than that. There was also the chance to bounce a basketball with Father Carl Hickey if I got there early enough, usually around 7 or so. Since the crowd seldom showed up until after eight, Father Carl would dig out the building's only aging basketball and run us for an hour. Wise young man that he was, he instinctively knew that the way to a teen's heart is sport, and that once the heart is reached, the soul is only a skip away.

Between the CYO and the priests' residence next door was a small `L-shaped skating rink. A fence protected it from

Waterloo and Cliff Streets, making it accessible only by the lane that separated the two buildings. Two or three times every winter we'd have a skating party in conjunction with the regular dance. The ice surface wasn't very large but when you remember that many of us had learned to skate at "the postage stamp", a tiny rink next to the old police station at Carmarthan and King Street East, it was Olympic.

Then there was the bowling alley on the ground floor, and the swimming pool where Fred Tobias taught us to swim, and that great running track that circled the gym floor itself. That's where we'd set up our "sound system", a 45 rpm turntable cranked as loud as the walls could stand.

The young people themselves fell into three categories. First of all there were the neophytes, the grade eight or nine kids there for the first time. They were easy to pick out because they'd stand against the wall in small groups of five or six, collars up, blatantly cool, chewing juicy fruit until their jaws ached. Always uneasy, maybe even confused, with the sexuality they were just discovering, they'd gawk enviously at the rhythmic gyrations of the older bunch. Then there were the grade tens and elevens, many of them temporarily secure in the company of their `steadies', singing to the music as they danced, convinced they were the envy of every eye in the gym. Finally there were the grade twelvers, the veterans, tenaciously (indeed smugly) confident in the social skills they were so certain they'd mastered. Their very movements belied their hubris; the guys would strut and the girls would glide, which made for some pretty ackward walks home.

Sometimes, usually around Christmas or Easter, some of the university crowd would drop by. They were easy to pick out because they never took off their college jackets. Sweating profusely, they'd wander freely around the gym, guys punching each other in the arm and girls exchanging theatric hugs, like Betty Davis was always so good at. They seemed a bit like fish out of water, almost a deja vu of when they had been grade eighters and here for the first time. Generally they'd show up once or twice, complain the crowd was too young for them, and join the older crowd at Lily Lake, anxiously searching for something they hadn't yet realized they'd lost. They would understand soon enough.

I had first met Father Carl just after he'd been ordained. We hit it off right away. I always found him really easy to talk to, more like someone my own age than a priest. Shortly after his ordination, he'd been put in charge of our Hi-Y group and was determined it would be THE place for teens to be on a Saturday night. Once or twice a week he'd meet with his young executive to plan special events still a month or so away. He was always gentle with us, coaching genuine leadership skills that would serve us well in the difficult decade just beyond each of our horizons. Of course, we had no idea he was doing all this. As far as we were concerned this was just fun stuff that got us into the dance for free, but Father Carl knew us better than we thought.

He was a tall man, very athletic. It was always reassuring to know he was nearby on those infrequent Saturday evenings when we could sense an altercation brewing. Usually a firm hand on the shoulder was enough to cool things sufficiently, but on the two or three occasions when Father Carl thought it necessary that someone be asked "to leave", there wasn't a lot the individual could do once the trip toward the door was in progress.

At the end of my first year of university I was driving down Waterloo Street when I saw Father Ed Gallagher on the way to his visits at the General Hospital. He looked quite tired so I stopped to offer him a lift the rest of the way. That's how I found out that Father Carl and his good friend Father Joe Leahy were missing on a fishing trip to Loch Lomond Lake. Not long after that they found both bodies.

The loss felt by the parish, especially the young people, was enormous. Personally I think it was the first time I ever associated someone's death with the adjectives "senseless" and "unfair". But as the clouds of anger slowly dispersed, I gradually came to realize how much I and countless other young people my age had benefited from our brief brush with Father Carl. It was more than the spiritual, as important as that was. When I remember him today, it isn't in priestly vestments saying mass or even with his clerical collar and black shirt. No, the image I have of Father Carl is in mid air, arm outstretched, t-shirt soaked, completing a picture-perfect lay-up on a Saturday evening in the CYO gym.

What I'm saying is this: before I met him my impression of the priests and nuns with whom and for whom I worked at church and at school was that they were somehow superhuman, characters of unflawed patience immune to those "human" frailties that the rest of us mortals had to wrestle with. Not Father Carl though. Sure he did all that priest stuff on a regular basis, but he also could dribble, and cast a fly, and laugh at a good joke, and have his darker moments, frustrations perhaps more frequent in his vocation than for most of us. Quite simply, he was mortal.

Before long I extended this awareness to other presences in my life. University professors, people at all levels of authority, even obnoxious know-it-alls became infinitely less intimidating once I reminded myself they're as human as I.

And through my years as a teacher, when someone wasn't measuring up to snuff, Father Carl was always there to remind me that the reverse, the secret of compassion, is equally true: I'm as human as they.

# *John Doiron*

*"Before Honour Is Humility"*

...Proverbs 15:33

Picking role models is as instinctive as imprinting. Sometimes we're not so fortunate and don't realize what's happened until the pain arrives; other times, we luck in.

The trap is obvious: we don't "choose" our heros in the same way we might pick a shirt or order from a menu. In truth, we have no idea it's even happening. We just cross paths, however innocently, with someone who for one reason or another strikes us as special, and the rest is as reflexive as thirst. It's only later, much later, warmed by the firefly glow of meditation, that we grasp our indebtedness, and by then, mortality being what it is, it's often too late for any benediction.

In 1950 I became an altar boy at the Cathedral. We lived just around the corner on Exmouth Street, so the Cathedral was a building with which I was more than passingly familiar. What I hadn't seen up close, however, was the open lot at the back, overlooking the Saint Vincent's school yard. A twenty foot incline was buttressed with a massive concrete retaining wall which also served as one of the boundaries of the cindered playground in the schoolyard below. Beyond and stretching toward Golding Street was the old Thistle Curling Club. Its massive roof, just a step below the farthest edge of the retaining wall, was the perfect `short cut' between Cliff and Golding, provided of course you didn't get caught.

There was a house there too. It sat at the top of the slope, immediately behind the vestry: a two-story, greenish building tucked into the far corner of a then painfully small parking lot.

I hadn't been an altar boy very long before I learned that this was where John lived. John was a kind of church sexton, charged with everything from ringing the bell at funerals to patching drafty windows. Monsignor Cronin and the other priests could say the masses and baptize the babies, but keeping God's house in order was John's commission, and he took the job very seriously. Early arrivals for the 6:45 morning mass would invariably find the door open and the lights on; John was on the job. In winter, the front steps were always shovelled and sanded; John again. And during lent, when there was a real demand for candles in the Virgin's Chapel, it was John who made sure the multi-tiered racks were never empty.

His shyness made him a difficult man to get to know. He was always nearby, but most of the time behind the altar or in the catacombs under the church. In time I learned his full name was John Doiron, that his family lived with him in the house out back, and that none of the other altar boys, even the oldest ones, could remember a time when he wasn't there.

Over the next four or five years, the fact that I lived on Exmouth street got me a lot more masses than most of the other guys. In addition to my regular spot on the Sunday rotation (we had five morning masses every Sunday), I drew a lot of funerals through the week. Most of them were from Fitzpatrick's across the street, and almost all were at a special 9:00 mass. Depending on whether the mass was `high' or `solemn high', anywhere from four to six of us were needed, though many mornings we had to make do with as few as three. Anyway, one of us would always station himself behind the altar near the door closest to the vestry area. A tiny hole had been bored through the wall at eye level, letting us watch the back door of the church for the arrival of the casket. Meanwhile, John would be at the side door below the bell tower waiting for the procession to emerge across the street.

As soon as the casket was carried out, John would pull mightily on a rope which dropped through the floor above him and the massive Cathedral bell would toll a single note. The exercise was repeated at fifteen or twenty second intervals until the deceased was carried through the front door of the church; then we'd take over. Led by the cross bearer and accompanied by the mournful strains of the "Dies ira", we'd march to the back for opening prayer. John would always be there, head bowed, standing respectfully just inside one of the side doors.

I know it's funny, but I can't remember what occasion there was for the two of us to strike up a friendship. Maybe I was attracted by his humility, by how faithful he was to the thousand and one little jobs that fell to him every day. He was always doing something. Not the Sistine Chapel kind of `something' that might leave you breathless with admiration; no, rather the very menial chores that we take for granted and sometimes assume get done by themselves, or even were always that way.

That's where John really shone: little things like replacing lights, checking electrical connections, locking up for the night. It seemed to me that these were his prayers, his private devotions, as meaningful to him as a rosary or a way of the cross. I can't say for sure he was a man of faith in the traditional sense; to tell the truth, I can't remember ever seeing him kneel. But if the Benedictine adage equating "work" with "prayer" has any validity, his fidelity was unassailable.

I don't remember John's dying. That's the way our individual universes always seem to unfold, I guess. To tell the truth, better than three decades passed without so much as a passing thought of him. Then, in 1983, in preparation for the one hundred and fiftieth anniversary of the building of the Cathedral, I had the opportunity to sit on a committee that oversaw the project. Over a span of better than a year, the venerable structure was restored to its original condition, with great pain taken to be as authentic as possible. During those months, as brick by brick it bathed in its own fountain of youth, I had lots of time to remember, and much to my surprise many of those memories were of John. I had no idea until then how much I had admired him.

When restoration was complete, I had the opportunity to speak on behalf of our committee. We gathered in the Virgin's Chapel (now Our Lady's Chapel) on a Sunday afternoon to celebrate all that had been accomplished. I spoke of how proud the original builders would have been to see what had been done. I noted the special pains which had been taken to restore rather than rebuild, and wondered aloud how many contented spirits were lurking peacefully in the thousand shadowed corners of its walls.

After I'd returned to my seat, I let my imagination take over. Bishops Bray and Leverman; Monsignor Cronin, Monsignor (then Father) Gallagher; Fathers Quinn, Riley and LeBlanc: dozens and dozens of men who had each played their own small parts molding what I call me. They were all there.

And in the middle of them, dressed in the same work clothes he wore at all those funerals, was John. His contented expression was the one I'd seen so many times after evening benediction when his day was all but done.

His house was definitely in order.

# *My First And Last Hanging*

When I was growing up I lived in separate two worlds. In the summer, at our summer camp, I was a country boy, as close to the earth as I would ever get, but for the rest of the year an urbanite through and through.

My summer life was totally different from my city one. It wasn't so much a conscious attempt to keep it that way; it just happened. The friends I had could be slotted into one life or the other but very rarely into both. Sometimes, like when three or four of the crowd from Exmouth Street would bike to the camp, the two would merge but I didn't like it when this happened. There was something unnatural about it, like a chemistry book on a lawn chair or a barbecue in the city.

An exception was John Walsh. John was a stockier than average kid with a great sense of humor, perfect teeth, and a buzz-cut long before it was the "in" thing. He was the adventurous one in our group, the one we always got to test things: new chocolate bars, the latest chewing gum, the strength of that iffy-looking limb with the big apples. I remember he was the one we convinced to take a first swallow of ginger beer. As it turned out it was also his last swallow of ginger beer and we took his word for it.

Now and then, though, John would surprise us. One late July afternoon, Jim Hope, John and I were sitting by the edge of the lake near Dolan's boathouse. It was John who first noticed the old jackshirt and pair of pants lying on the grass below the veranda.

"Who ya' think left that stuff there." It was more of an observation than a question, but there wasn't much else to consider on a hot afternoon so we gave it a chance.

John continued. "Too bad it's not Halloween. We could make a dummy or something and hang it from a tree". Pause. "Scare the pants off some little kid." He waddled across the grassy slope in perfect imitation of a pre-schooler with pants around his knees.

Jim jumped at the thought. "It doesn't have to be Halloween! We can do it tonight, after dark." He stumbled to his feet and reached for the dirty overalls. "It'll be a cinch! We could get some old boots and an old hat, and tie some rope around the neck, and hang it from..."

The plan had met its first hurdle. Now that we were getting organized, where would we go with it.

"...the mill window!" Jim's tone sounded like he'd just discovered Archimedes' principle or something. "We could hang it from the front window so it's over the road! It'll be great!"

A vote wasn't necessary.

For the next few hours we laboured in the darkness of the garage below the camp, door closed to avoid detection. A half hour before sunset we had a dummy worthy of an Academy Award. Wads of newspaper Dad had been saving for whenever he might get around to painting the front room, stuffed into overalls and shirt. An old hunting cap perched on a nylon-stockinged head. And the coup de grace, a pair of over-sized and well-worn sneakers used for working around the lawn. A splash of ketchup on the chest and it was complete. Perfection.

To escape detection we lugged our creation along the edge of the brook that paralleled the road. The mill itself, abandoned years before, had weathered well, but time and more than a little pilfering had taken their toll. All that remained was a shell, three barren floors, and a community of bats that regimentally deserted the place each evening at sunset.

The northern end came to within a few yards of the main road. An upstairs window would be the perfect spot for our hanging. It would be easy enough to get there since all the doors had long ago been removed to serve as walls in any of a thousands "forts" we'd built over the years. Darkness growing, we made our way to the top floor three stories up. A length of two-by-four from the garage became our gallows. From the end, tethered by about six feet of rope, dangling above the road, we suspended our dummy. Then outside to see how it looked.

By now a three-quarter moon was beginning to compensate for the deepening shadows, and a slight breeze held off since morning by the heat of the day was approaching from the Bay of Fundy ten miles or so to the south. The mill itself was assuming its nighttime reality, little more than a silhouette bordered by purple sky. We surveyed our creation and could immediately see that it would most certainly do. Any little kid unfortunate enough to happen by would drop his drawers for sure.

On the side of the road opposite the mill was a fairly steep slope of perhaps fifteen feet capped by heavy alders bordering the woods beyond. Here we sat, giggling like two-year olds, excited as cloggers at a Little Jimmy Dickens concert, and waited.

Mrs. Burke (the name is assumed, needless to say) was definitely overweight. She was as close to being circular as any human could be. Very conscious of her enormity, she was seldom seen in the light of day unless wearing a blanket or something. Her habit was to stay inside, where it was obviously cooler, until late evening. Only then would she emerge to sit at the picnic table in front of her house or suffer the thirty-minute walk down the road to Daley's Grocery Store and Service Station. During the daytime she was quite happy just to snack and read, and her favourite reading was really scary stories, the weirder the better. All day long she would escape to a world of dismemberment and decapitation, and if her daughter was to be believed, her nightmares were just as gory.

By the time she'd stuffed tomorrow's snacks into grocery bags and exchanged recent gossip it was pitch dark. Jim was the first to catch sight of her as she came around the bend. Right away we knew who it was. No one else moved like she did. It was for all the world like each foot wanted to go in a different direction and her body just dragged along between.

We couldn't tell for sure when it was she first realized something was out of place. About twenty feet from the mill she stopped humming and seemed to slow down just a bit. The figure above, backlit by the high moon and a glow from camps surrounding the nearby lake, twisted and moved with a slight pendulum motion.

Mrs. Burke stopped, eyes straight ahead, immobile for about ten seconds. She seemed to sense something was out of place even before she knew what or where. A half turn let her check for anyone that might be following her. Nothing. She cocked an ear to the nearby forest. Still nothing. By now she was facing her original direction again, unnerved by an instinctive certainty that something was definitely wrong. Then slowly, very slowly, she began to tilt her head, inch by inch, inch by inch, until she was looking straight up at the figure's feet. We steeled ourselves for the inevitable scream. It didn't come. In its place, the "thunk" and then "thunk" again of grocery bags sliding one after another to the ground. For maybe ten more seconds she stood: empty-armed, stone-still, eyes fixed on the shape above her and the night sky beyond. Then, she began to run! We couldn't believe it. Mrs Burke was actually running! But it wasn't a real run. It was as if each foot headed for opposite sides of the road and the rest of her just wanted to get out of there at any cost, like Leacock's description of jumping on a horse and riding off in all directions. Before we knew it she was gone, swallowed up by the darkness with never so much as a whimper.

When we were sure she was well on her way we slid down the embankment to the road. We'd figured on a better than even chance to scare some little kid, but Mrs. Burke! It began to dawn on us what a great thing we had here, and we were going to milk it for whatever it was worth. When a car came by a few minutes later we stood ankle-deep in weeds on the shoulder of the road and pointed upward, trying our darnest to look terrified. It must have worked because the car swerved a bit and then accelerated into the night.

Now we were really pumped!

Another car! Let's do it again. With each new passer-by we were more and more delirious: yelling, pointing, gesticulating wildly.

After a half dozen or so vehicles we sat on the embankment and caught our breath. We couldn't even talk, we were so excited. This was better than spinning the bottle!

"Here's another one coming!" Jim was on his feet and at the edge of the road when we noticed that this car was a little different from the others. It was that little red light that suddenly appeared on its roof!

John stopped in his tracks and spun around, all in one motion.

"The Mounties!"

Time to exit! Only one way: the woods beyond the brook, but getting there wouldn't be easy. A few yards of raspberry bushes, four or five feet of shallow water, and then an alder grove that would scare a lumberjack, and all the while the awful awareness of that little red light pulsing at the edge of the road.

By the time we'd reached the relative safety of the woods we were a pretty scratched up and thoroughly saturated threesome but we still had the presence of mind to know we'd make less noise if we separated. Jim headed upstream, which was quite logical since he LIVED upstream, but John and I had a tougher row to hoe. We worked our way through the woods to the lake, circled the shoreline, and crossed the road as quickly as possible. When we finally reached the security of the camp, we were quite content just to sit for the next few hours with the lights out.

It was a week or so before our wounds healed. I told my parents that I'd fallen into a blackberry bush, which got me a ton of sympathy but didn't help the itch go away. There's a positive spin to the whole episode though. I made a resolution that night which I've been faithful to for forty years: that was my first and last hanging.

# *Gone Fishin'*

When I was a kid being brought up in the East End, I was reasonably content with my lot in life. Acres of backyard to roam through, more than enough rocks to throw, tons of friends, Saturday afternoon movies; but I must confess one pastime I did begrudge my rural counterparts: fishing!

I guess it was because my father was such a fishing nut that I too got hooked (no pun!). Time and again he'd come home from a trip to Loch Lomond Lake with soon to be developed pictures of enormous brownies he and his buddy, Billy Madill, had caught that weekend. Even better, he'd bring home a fish or two for me to see and proudly bring out the old Kodak to capture the memory on our front steps. I remember vividly how hefty they were and how tough it was to hold them high enough to avoid tails touching the ground. Then and there I knew that some day, some how, I had to catch one of those for myself.

When my parents bought our summer camp in the mid-fifties, the first thing I had to know was if there was a lake nearby. No lake, I announced, and they could count me out! Well O.K., so I didn't actually SAY that, but I sure thought it loud enough! I needn't have worried though. It was a beauty, the perfect place not only for fishing but for swimming, rowing, rock skipping, even tiny-turtle hunting. Within a week I had my first rod and reel, complete with a package of assorted hooks, a couple of sinkers (which I never did figure out how to use) and a red and white plastic bobber to let me know when the marlin took the bait. If memory serves me true, my first catch was a floppy little sunfish about two inches long, but it was a start!

From grade six to grade twelve I enthusiastically fished my summers away ...usually alone, with just my lake or brook for company... but university years dampened my youthful eagerness. Summers were now measured in eight hour shifts at Bathurst Containers, which didn't leave a lot of time for wetting a line. Sure, I got out a few times, but for all intents and purposes my fishing career was put on hold for four years.

When I finally did get around to rescuing rod and reel, I was surprised to find that one element had quietly changed. It wasn't much fun to fish alone anymore, and the nature experience, those trees, old roads, and brooks with little bridges, had quietly assumed a major role in determining what degree of satisfaction a day's adventure might be worth. Without any conscious consideration on my part, where I fished had become as important as what I might eventually catch, and the fact that the whole experience was shared with a kindred spirit made the day more memorable still.

From then on I never fished alone. When I escaped it was always with someone, and it's only in the last few years that I'm really beginning to reap the rewards of remembering together.

Two stories come to mind immediately. Ironically both memories originated in almost the same spot, though years apart. The setting was Adams Lake, not far from the farmhouse where my father was born and raised. A serenely quiet place in the shape of a painter's palette edged with soft evergreens and gentle stands of alder, it was and still is the stuff sonnets are made of. At its mouth, a miniscule waterfall no more than a couple of feet deep empties into a brook which leads to other lakes and another brooks, and then the river and finally the bay and beyond. Whenever I visit there, close to my roots, I'm struck by the realization that nature, like heredity, is so orderly, so symbiotic. Some days the experience verges on religious.

My first memory is of a late spring afternoon when Barb and I were going together but not yet engaged. I had often ranted about this great fishing spot I knew, and how I was guaranteed at least one good fish with as little as five minutes investment. Finally Barb had heard the story more than enough and decided to call my hand. We threw a rod and a few worms into the trunk and off we went on the half hour drive to the mouth of the lake. I really don't think she had a lot of faith we'd have any luck, especially when she got a look at the piddling little brook itself.

For whatever reason (probably unbridled doubt!) she waited in the car while I made my way to the foot of the little waterfall; we were close enough to the road that she could see me all the way anyway. I must admit the pool looked disappointingly shallow when I reached it but I tossed a hook in anyway and waited.

I didn't have to wait for long. A fierce tug almost pulled me into the shallows around the edge, and thirty seconds later I was the proud owner of a pound-and-a-half trout. From a pool no more than four feet wide! And it didn't stop there either! Before I left we caught another one about the same size! Barb was proud of me! I was proud of me! I was a hero, and there's no greater satisfaction than being a hero to the lady you hope to marry, though in secret moments I've had this nagging question whether it was I or the fish who finally won her.

My second remembrance was set a decade and a half later and might need a note of explanation. Year after year I took pride in the brag that I never missed the first day of fishing season. Yes, it was usually pretty cold, and sure, more times than I can count I came home fishless, but some macho ritual demanded I be there, frostbite or not. Some years the spring thaw came early and the mouth of the brook was already clear when we arrived opening morning. Most years though we had lots of work to do before the actual fishing started.

I remember the April Saturday when Terry Comeau and I slogged our way through a couple of feet of snow to get to the top edge of the lake. It was a really cold morning and the ice was tight to the shore. Our options were perfectly clear: either we break through to the water beneath or we go home. We chose the former.

From the nearby woods we retrieved an old birch log that would do fine as a ice-breaker-througher. Then for the next hour we pounded, pried, pushed and swore until we had created an opening about six feet in diameter. Then we dug out whatever it was we were using as bait, bacon rind I think it was, and (as our fishing buddy Joe Breen used to say) "fished hard".

But `fish hard' as we did, there wasn't so much as a nibble: not even a curious minnow. After two or three hours had passed we were getting pretty discouraged. It was definitely time for some rationalizing here.

"You know, I don't think the fish are bitin' at all. Maybe it's too early yet."

"Water's still too cold."

"Probably didn't help with all that ice whacking either."

"Just a waste of time with all this snow."

That's when the kid on the bike arrived. I swear, two feet of snow and all, he arrived on a bike. And the little twerp didn't even say hello! All he did was set down the bike, walk out along the edge of the pool, OUR pool, take a piece of fluff off his jacket, put it on his hook, and that was that. Three minutes later he left with the nicest fish either of us had seen in a long time!

There oughta be a law!

# *Exmouth Street*

Every neighbourhood has at least one of them: a relatively private place where the local kids go for harmless fun. It might be a ball field, or maybe even a cultivated Square or piece of park resplendent with benches and picnic tables, perhaps even some trees. For those of us on Exmouth Street in the late forties and early fifties, there were two such havens: the Green Hill, and Hazen's Castle.

The Green Hill still sits where it always did at the foot of the street where Exmouth drops suddenly to what once was Prince Edward but is now Brunswick Drive. It's a weathered, rocky outcrop capped with thick grass on its crest and sides. There used to be a weedy growth around its base too but for reasons that always escaped me the turf there never seemed as lush as the stuff at the top. In between were tiers of rock made for climbing. Every foot or so brought a new ledge just wide enough to cling to, or another notch made to fit small hands perfectly.

Each season carried its own favourite Green Hill game. In the Spring, to kids more than a little fired up because of the long winter's cloister, it was climbing time. We'd gather at the bottom, choose up teams of two or three, and away we'd go, the first to the top claiming bragging rights for a few minutes at least. In Summer, fresh from a World War none of us understood, it was shoot-em-up games; soldiers, cowboys, indians and federal agents; even the occasional extra-terrestrial roamed the summit, personifications of forces good and evil that existed well beyond our block but visited The Green Hill only in our imaginations. In autumn, especially when it got dark right right after supper, it was time for flashlight tag, a game that could on a good night extend all the way up the street to the alley beside Mr. MacFadyen's store.

Early January was the best time though. During New Year's week we'd search front steps and back yards for discarded Christmas trees. Whatever we found, we'd drag it to the top of The Green Hill to add to the pile, and when we had enough we'd put together the greatest forts you ever saw. Fir trees were the best but we didn't quibble over the occassional spruce either. Properly threaded together they also made great landing spots after a dare-devil run and flying leap.

Good, harmless games, for the most part the inventions of the kids who played them in a time when Meccano sets were as technological as you could get. All that was necessary was The Green Hill and a child or two with time or their hands.

The other stop on our version of the Magical Mystery Tour was Hazen's Castle. It sat at the end of Hazen Street where Saint Joseph's Hospital is today. High on the hill above City Road it offered a spectacular view from Fort Howe Hill almost to Haymarket Square. The quickest way to get there was along Golding Street. This led to an aldered slope behind the curling rink adjacent to the Hazen's Castle property. It wasn't really a castle but it was as close as those of us from Exmouth would ever get to a real one. Personally I never got up enough courage to look in a window; the alder bushes were as far as I dared go for fear some fierce gardener with a two-day beard and a missing tooth might capture me and turn me into mulch. I left that to the braver ones among us, and they assured me it was well worth the risk: old suits of armour, swords and shields hanging from the walls, and even an odd torture rack. And there were even rumours of ghosts! I believed every word.

Hazen's Castle was more than just a house on a hill though. To the right, about half way down the grade between the Castle and the General Hospital, was a little pen that held four or five fat sheep. Given this was in the middle of the city, it was quite an attraction, kind of like our own mini-zoo. Whenever a day really started to drag, a trip to `the sheep place' was always good for an hour or so. With a bit of luck we might wrangle enough out of our parents for a bag of chips and a bottle of pop (fifteen cents would be plenty) and turn the trip into a picnic of sorts. There on the side of the hill we'd sit, making sheep noises and lamenting that something so shaggy had to become a sweater some day. As for the sheep, I think they enjoyed us as much as we did them. They'd gather at the side of the fence and poke noses through the links to lick the salt from our hands.

Hazen's Castle is long gone now and I haven't seen a decently fed sheep since they tore the pen down fifty years ago. The Green Hill's still there though. Sure, it's aged a bit, but not nearly as much as the kids who used to play there. Every month or so I find a solid excuse to drive down Exmouth. Half the houses of my childhood are gone and the street seems a lot narrower and definitely shorter. Urban renewal has taken its toll to the south and the stately profile of the old General Hospital has disappeared. But from a vantage point at the bottom of the hill behind Romero House, it's only a scant warp in time to happier, less complicated days when being a kid was so much easier.

*Chopping Onions*

# *Elizabeth's Bible*

You can tell just by looking that it's very old. The front cover is no longer attached, the victim of some household accident decades ago, but despite the mutilation that bible sits today with hallowed dignity on an end table in our living room.

It had been a gift to my Great-Aunt Elizabeth Lynch when she was still very young, the moment captured forever on an early page: "Presented to Lisa M. Lynch by her mother, November 23, 1885".

When Elizabeth finally died at age 89 in July of 1964, she was the last of her family. She had chosen never to marry and her final decade or two had been spent living with us. I must admit that my personal time with her was to a large extent wasted because I was too young to sense any real need to know her. I was twenty-two the summer she passed away but four of those twenty-two years had been spent away from home and another two or three of them caught up in the excitement of high school and adolescence. Consequently any genuine time we'd enjoyed had been limited to maybe ten years and, young as I was, questions that surfaced after her death had yet to occur.

Nonetheless it had been a marvelous relationship: warm, sharing, sometimes even humorous, like the time she mistook a wedge of ExLax for a candy bar. Other moments were much more complex, like when she answered the phone and started to cry because my grandfather had passed away. It didn't occur to me at the time that my grandfather was her only surviving brother.

She was a tiny lady, made to appear all the tinier by the dowager's hump that left her perpetually bent forward, but she had an inner strength born of enough suffering and sacrifice to fit three lifetimes. When I started teaching mythology in junior high school one of my favourite heros was Atlas, bent over by his burden of the world; his plight made me think of Elizabeth.

For reasons no doubt private to herself she seldom mentioned her brothers and sisters to me when I was young. Thanks to my mother I knew that there was Aunt Mary O'Donnell who lived in the big white house across from the Catholic church in Dipper Harbour, and I always just assumed that she'd had a mother and father at some time or other, but these and other questions passed by as quickly as they'd appeared and answers were never pursued.

Mom always had insisted that I was Elizabeth's favourite person in the world so when she died I inherited the big bible that had sat on the sidetable by her bed for as long as she had been with us. Many an evening I'd wandered into her room with some discovery or other only to find her gently leafing the pages, reading a text here and another there, revisiting close friends.

I certainly cherished it from the moment it was given to me but I must admit it was some time, years even, before I really opened it and took a good look. I was into roots pretty heavily at the time and I wanted to know more about my mother's side of the family, Elizabeth in particular.

That's when I discovered a moment captured forever in time, defying even death. On the first page of the preface, etched in the handwriting of a young girl not yet fifteen. was the inscription, "17th of August, 1890, Sunday, quarter after three".

For a moment I was stunned. The Elizabeth I had known had been an old woman, but here on the page in front of me was a young lady I'd never met, sitting with her bible a century before. Who had she been? What things truly mattered to her? What thoughts were running through her young girl mind that Sunday afternoon?

Part of the answer I discovered in the middle of the book on a page that recorded the death dates of brothers and sisters I'd never realized she's had.

"John Lynch, died June 14, aged 16, 1884

Nellie E. McLaughlin, died Sept. 7, aged 21, 1888"

The young lady I was discovering had already lost a brother and sister and she was little more than half way through her teens. What had been on her adolescent mind was becoming all too clear.

But the real tragedy was yet to come. Three months and a few days later:

Patrick G. Lynch, died Nov. 26, aged 18, 1890"

And the next entry:

"Margeretta G. Lynch, died Aug. 18, aged 18, 1891"

In the space of five years she'd lost three brothers and two sisters between the ages of sixteen and twenty-six, a tragic half decade that must have been overwhelming. For the first time in my life I was coming to grasp with just who Elizabeth was: not a frail, elderly person who had always been that way, but a human being who'd laughed and cried, rejoiced and agonized like we all must. My love for her had taken on a new dimension.

I don't think my relationship with Elizabeth was all that unique. Many of us have elderly mothers and fathers, uncles and aunts whom, through our own omission, we fail to know. The loss is our own. Immeasurable well-springs of wisdom and experience lie untapped simply because we're in too big a hurry to slow down and listen. It's a middle-age conceit that we mistake aging for senility and miss the essential reality of life itself: that wisdom is the Almighty's compensation for growing old; that age has little to do with youth and nothing whatsoever to do with common sense.

I was with Elizabeth the hour before she left us. The last she spoke to me was an affirmation of the enormous faith that had kept her young for eighty-nine years: "I'll be waiting for you."

And I have no doubt she will. But this time we'll sit down and really talk. There's so much I have to know.

# *Moments In Time*

We all have those moments in our lives that we associate with a specific instant in time. In most cases they're incidents that have occurred in the last half century because before the early 1960's, news took a little longer to get from there to here, the effect of which was an emotional cushion buffering us from any immediacy in either time or place.

With the advent of the "global village", however, all of this changed. No longer were momentous and sometimes terrifying events relegated to the past or to somewhere "over there"; the advent of satellite television reduced everything to the here and now, and brought to our doorsteps and indeed dinner tables the painful immediacy of reality.

It's easy to identify the images. For me, the first was Dallas. An empty Lincoln convertible sitting in front of Parkland Hospital, surrounded by hundreds of men and women with their hands over their mouths in a posture of disbelief. Lee Harvey Oswald being shot while the world watched in cathartic horror. A very young John Kennedy Jr. saluting the coffin that carried his assassinated father. Later there would be Vietnam napalm, the Chicago Convention and the Watts riots; earthquakes and grass fires; plane crashes, burning buildings, the bombing of Iraq and the death of a Princess, each accessible in the relative comfort of one's living room.

In an ironic sort of way, all of this was anticipated in a popular television show of the late 1950's called "You Are There". Hosted by Walter Cronkite, the premise was a trip back in time to great moments of history where we would be present at the Battle of Hastings, the trial of Jesus or the death of Julius Caesar. Little could Cronkite have foreseen that terrible moment on November 22, 1963 when, struggling to maintain his composure, it would fall on his shoulders to announce to the world that the president had died.

In sober moments, we find ourselves considering the implications of such accessibility. Particularly in the cyberspace age of the twenty-first century, it behooves us to seek within for our human motives. Why do we find such carnage so fascinating? Is it in the name of information gathering, predicated on the mistaken assumption that unbridled awareness will eliminate ignorance? Or maybe it's a purging, a modern way to excrete the darker compulsions that are the residue of our animal heritage; a cleansing of sorts, where we seize the opportunity to point the finger of guilt at someone other than ourselves.

Or is it something far more sinister and menacing than any of these.

Great empires have preceded us: the Hittites, the Egyptions, the Greeks and the Romans. As different as each was from its predecessor, they all had one quality in common: their fall was marked by a philosophical and religious decay characterized by the breakdown of family, blatant disregard for the dignity of the human condition, and resulting acts of inhumanity on a scale unprecedented in that empire's "golden age".

It will be up to generations still decades away to decide when the twentieth century ended for our Western World. Will the benchmark moment be November 22, 1963? Will it be a moment specific to the Technological Revolution brought on by the computor age? Or is the fateful event still hidden around a corner yet to be turned? In any case, now is the perfect time for each of us and for humankind in general to ponder where we've been, what we are, and where the future might take us.

# *"A Fool And His Money Are Soon Parted"*

...English Proverb

Embarrassment can be a character builder, but it's big brother, Mortification, can reduce you to a snivelling idiot.

When I was in high school, the uptown area was the heartbeat of Saint John. The closest thing to a "mall" was the Fairview Plaza, a bus ride away (or a pretty good walk at least), and McAllister and Parkway were still a gleam in some contractor's eye. As a matter of fact, I can vividly recall helping Smith Cathline hay a good-sized piece of marshland on the corner of Westmorland Road and McAllister Drive, just where Parkway is today. Not even Forest Hills had been invented yet.

No, uptown was definitely the place to be. Whatever one's heart desired was to be found in a area bounded by Prince William, Princess, Carmarthan and Union, with the southern end of Waterloo thrown in for good measure.

Life began at the Mayfair Theater where a goodly number of my Saturday afternoons were spent with Hoppy, Roy, Gene, Lash, Cisco, et al. I didn't keep count, but I'll bet I saw dozens of versions of the death of Billy The Kid, no two of them the same.

A half block farther was Duvall's Hardware Store. At the rear of the main floor, a double staircase led upstairs to where toys were arrayed. When I was younger, my favourite spot was the display with those great Daisy air-rifles and holster sets. Later on, after I discovered fishing and baseball, I took to hanging around downstairs, just inside the front door, drooling over those new spinning reels and shiny Spalding catcher's mitts that shared the same display case.

And there were dozens of places like these: Woolworth's, Louie Green's, Zellers, the MRA building, Pascal Emerson, and the list goes on. At Christmas time, the excitement was electric.

One special Saturday I particularly remember. It was an unusually hot summer afternoon. I'd spent the morning scouring our neighbourhood for pop bottles and cashing them in. A couple of hours sweat and a broken piggy bank had left me with almost seven dollars, much more than I'd need to buy that 'hulla popper' spinning lure in Duvall's window. But when I got to the store, the popper was gone.

"You gettin' any more in?"

The heavy-set man behind the counter obviously felt bad for me. He wasn't the guy who usually took care of the sports counter so he didn't know me from Adam, but you could still tell he felt bad. That didn't help a lot though. There was nothing he could do.

"Sorry, that's the last one. And I doubt we'll get more in now. Season's almost over."

He reached into the display case.

"What about this minnowy thing here. Don't it look real!" He wiggled a ridiculous piece of plastic across the counter top.

Twenty minutes later I was sitting in Kings Square across the street from Woolworth's feeling really sorry for myself. I must have looked particularly pathetic because one elderly lady stopped to feel my forehead and ask if I was feeling alright. When I assured her I was fine, she wasn't totally convinced, so she reached into her purse and handed me a dime.

"Here. Get yourself a pop or something. You'll feel better then."

That's when it hit me. What's the good of seven dollars if you're not willing to spend it, and uptown was most certainly the place to be with seven dollars to spend.

The next hour and a half is still a bit of a blur. I do

74

remember the pop and chips at Green's, the peanut butter sand-wich at the Driscoll's Drug Store restaurant and the hamburger and fries (with gravy) at the Woolworth's canteen. To round off the splurge, a large popcorn, an O'Henry, and a movie at the Paramount.

Life was good.

I can't recall what was playing, but I do remember the unusually large crowd at the theater that day. It was so large that I couldn't get my usual spot up in the balcony and had to settle for a middle-of-the-row seat in the center section towards the front. As a matter of fact, I was so close to the screen I had to look up and squint a bit to see the picture. But the popcorn was hot, the butter was thick, and the O'Henry was as sticky as sticky could be.

Alimentary heaven.

It wasn't very long into the show, just after the cartoon I think, that I got my first hint something might be wrong. A sort of knawing in the pit of my stomach; kind of a dull ache. I shift-ed my weight and convinced myself it was nothing serious and I'd be great in a few minutes. But I wasn't great in a few min-utes. The knaw had a partner. An unmistakable lump was gath-ering in my throat and I was starting to feel chilly. After a half hour I was finally forced to face the truth: I was going to be sick... right here, over all these strangers... if I didn't get out right away.

I looked to my right: fifteen heads and thirty sprawling legs between me and the aisle. The left was no more promising. Either way, it wasn't going to be very graceful. Graceful or not, though, there was no other way. Holding my breath with all my might, I rose to my feet and headed for the horizon. It wasn't very pretty: flying hats, crushed toes, more than a few bruised cheek bones. One little kid was particularly wimpy when I sent his popcorn flying, but nothing was going to stop me now. The closer I got to the aisle, the more confident I got. My stomach was churning, but I was going to survive this one after all.

Thank you God, thank you.

Finally, after what seemed more like twenty hours than twenty seconds, I reached the aisle. And then, ...

Did I mention that I was an altar boy at the Cathedral for ten years.

And then, with five hundred pairs of eyes glued on my person..., yes, right then, with an elegance that would have moved even the Pope himself, I turned to the screen, bowed my head, ... and genuflected.

No sooner had my knee touched the floor than the whole theater erupted. Not with a polite snicker or even a subdued chuckle; no, far more thunderous than that. Even the ushers were leaning against the back wall, holding their splitting sides as I ran for the door.

And that wasn't the end of it. The next day I was scheduled to serve the 11:45 mass and was in the vestry hanging up my coat when Father Leahy strolled in. He had this weird smile on his face as he walked over and put his hand on my shoulder.

"Enjoy the movie?"

I served for Father Leahy many times after that until his untimely passing in the early `60's. He was a great guy and I really liked him. But I never did get used to the way he'd cover his face with his hand and look the other way whenever I genuflected.

# Mr. Gibson

### "Music Is The Thing Of The World I Love Most"

...Samuel Pepys

I don't think it cost very much, maybe fifteen or twenty dollars without a case, but in the eyes of a fourteen-year old, it was beautiful. Balanced among the lower branches, it stood tall among the other gifts awaiting harvest that Christmas morning, and I knew right away how I'd be spending my time until school re-opened in a week or so.

It all went back to the night I'd been doing my home-work in front of our newly acquired, single channel, black and white Sylvania, the first television we owned. This wasn't where I normally struggled with academics but the novelty of "moving pictures" in the house was still fresh enough to coax the entire family (and a half dozen neighbourhood friends) to share a hour or two in the twelve by twelve we called a living room. My mother and father must have sensed it was about time I experienced social occasions such as these so I was given dispensation to join the crowd.

Anyway, the show was a "musical visit" with the Dorsey Brothers, Tommy and Jimmy, and some "special friends" who'd fill three or four guest spots each week. I'd be hard-pressed today to name you the other three who appeared that night, but the fourth I'll never forget: a very young but supremely confident Elvis himself. What Dorsey fans saw was later to be "vintage Elvis": curled lip, impish smile, one strand of hair on the forehead, and more energy than a solar flare. The King had arrived.

The next day every teenage boy in North America became an Elvis clone. We dressed like him, talked like him, combed like him, sneered like him. And hundreds of thousands of us wanted something else, too... the final accessory that would make our transformation complete: a guitar. Mom and Dad, no doubt encouraged that their eldest was asking for something other than an air rifle, promised to do what they could. After all, who ever heard of someone's losing an eye to a guitar.

For the first few days I just held it, `cradled' it really. It didn't have a shoulder strap so I had to do my cradling sitting down, but for hours I'd experiment with plucking and strumming just to see what sounds I could coax. The first important step was to learn how to tune it. I knew it HAD to be tuned, but I had no idea HOW! An instruction book I found at Ben Goldstein's Music Store solved that problem; I was on my way to stardom.

Then one evening I made an amazing discovery: a few really simple songs, like the Peter Gunn Theme, could be played using just one string. Pick in hand, up and down the neck I squeaked until something remotely resembling Peter Gunn could be detected through the cacophony. When I first played it for my parents, they applauded vigorously and observed it was the best "Silent Night" they'd ever heard, but I wasn't discouraged. Time was on my side.

Shortly after that, for reasons I really can't remember (frustration, maybe), my guitar got set aside for awhile. By the time I entered university, the folk era was blossoming madly and a few of the guys on my floor could actually play, so I resurrected my old friend and gave it another try. This time I was infinitely more successful. Within a month or so I had mastered the `C', `F' and `G' chords and could bluff a dozen different songs. Then on to minor chords and other keys, and before long I was getting pretty good, at least enough to stand my own in your average second-floor sing-along. Every evening we'd get together in someone's room and wail our hearts out until only one of us was still awake.

When I invested in an electric and an amplifier a year or so later, I even entertained the thought of starting a band (I mean, isn't that how the Kingston Trio began?), but none of us could sing worth a damn and my playing was C+ at best, so we shelved that one pretty quickly. Besides, those were the days when universities had that lights-out policy; total blackness descended promptly at eleven. A bunch of us would still head for the washroom, the only spot on our floor where a bulb burned after curfew, but that was only half the fun because there was no plug for the amp and we could hardly hear the guitar without one.

When I started working and got my inaugural pay-cheque, the first place I went to was Goldstein's. On the wall were a dozen shiny Gibsons and I was about to move up. I picked one of the smaller models, more folksy than western (carrying case included). I remember I had the same feelings that day as I'd had that Christmas morning so many years before, but within a year I was ready to trade again, this time to a sweet-smelling J-45, the only one he had in the store.

A problem was developing though. My relationship with the guitar was beginning to resemble the affinity between a stamp collector and his stamps. I was getting more caught up with the instrument than with the music and I think I spent more time polishing than playing.

What happened next was inevitable. My boyhood friend and I drifted apart again. For better than a year that J-45 sat idle in its case in a corner near the foot of my bed. Then, thirty-five years ago when I first met the person I would marry and found out how much she liked to sing, it was only natural that Mr. Gibson and I would renew our acquaintance. At first it was difficult. Fingers had to be calloused all over again, and some of those chords that had been second nature to me a few years before seemed impossible stretches this time around. I stayed with it though and before long I was starting to feel comfortable once more. I even took the time to learn some new stuff:

Lightfoot, Cat Stevens and the like. By the time our first child arrived three years later, I was more confident with my music than I'd ever been. There was an added bonus too: nothing inspired a baby to drift into sleep like the quiet strumming of a guitar.

Next to Murphy's Law though, one of life's greatest frustrations is that, when you least expect it, stuff always seems to get in the way. Other distractions entered my life and for a third time my amigo and I drifted apart. This time it lasted for well over a decade, until the early eighties when our third child joined the family. There had been a break of eleven years since his sister had been born so it took quite an adjustment to get back to changing diapers, warming bottles and remembering all those great lullabies that had worked so well the first time around.

That's when old faithful re-entered the picture. Times had changed, but children hadn't. Three verses of "Love Me Tender" had him snoring peacefully every time. My childhood companion was home again. It wasn't any easier though; if anything, getting my fingers in shape and trying to remember what had once been second nature to me verged on being painful. I didn't give up though, and would you believe history repeated itself. Like my return years before, I discovered new songs and new chords; progressions that a decade ago had seemed impossible were finally there.

I guess that's the way all of life's connections are. We drift together and apart and together again, caught in the timeless ebb and flow of human relationships, discovering and rediscovering that whatever is worth having is worth working at.

And every time, the reward is greater than before.

Today, Mr. Gibson sits in his own warm corner. We visit as often as we can.

# *On Horses and Islands*

When John Donne observed, "No man is an island", I'm sure he'd also concede most of us would love to own one just the same.

Some isolated yet beautiful spot, the perfect place for visiting but not staying. A proverbial "get-away": sans phone, sans television, sans newspaper and Canada Post, with the greenest of grass and the gentlest of breezes.

Trouble is, not many of us will likely ever be in a position to get one so we have to carry on just the same, occasionally creating our own personal little islands in the billows of our imaginations.

In the summer of 1997 I was in Georgetown, Guyana doing some basketball stuff. As fascinating as was the trip itself, there was also a down side to the visit. The temperature seldom dropped below 35 and on a couple of days it broke into the early 40's. The visit called for four hours of open-air classroom each morning followed by observing basketball referees doing their thing through the afternoon.

The catch to this scenario is that basketball in Georgetown is normally played on outdoor courts: outdoor, unshaded courts with the nearest drinkable water a horizon away.

So it was that I found myself in the top row of a rusted outdoor bleacher, sweating profusely and hotter than a crustacean at a clam bake, as the most actionless of games unfolded in front of me. The sun was so bright not even my sunglasses kept me from squinting and as the contest wore on I found myself yearning for the cool breezes of my imaginary island.

Then the horse appeared.

It had wandered over from a nearby field only to find its path interrupted by the rectangular concrete of the basketball

court. On the other side and across the street was a good-sized tree with an inviting patch of shadow and that's where Mr. Horse was intent on going.

Oblivious to the commotion around him, he slowly meandered across the court, along a sideline and on to his island of shade. What amazed me more than anything else was the reaction (or rather the lack of reaction) of everyone at the game. While I searched frantically for my camera to capture the incongruity of the moment, the game carried on as if absolutely nothing were occurring. The players played, the refs "reffed", the fans alternately cheered and booed to the athletic gyrations of their local heroes.

And the world continued to unfold as it was meant to.

It later struck me how compatible each of us is with that Georgetown horse. When the spirit moves us, we can raise in an instant unseen yet impenetrable ramparts that block out everyone and everything around us. Driving a busy highway and suddenly realizing we're a mile or two farther than we expected to be, with no memory whatsoever of having passed a familiar landmark; awakening suddenly from what seems an appreciable

distance to the voice of a co-worker in what has apparently been a lengthy monologue that now demands a comment in reply.

We all need our space. As wonderful as it might be to be blessed with the ability to communicate, there are those inevitable moments when communicating is at the bottom of our "to do" list, when the warm fuzziness of losing oneself in meandering contemplation is about as good as it gets.

If we're lucky enough to have a real island in the vicinity we head straight for it; but when necessity dictates, we can do some pretty smooth improvising. It's my personal suspicion that our truly monumental epiphanies happen more often in washrooms than boardrooms; that a long walk is a worthwhile preface to heavy words; that more prayers are said in darkness than in the light of a thousand candles.

And answered too.

*Chopping Onions*

# *On Hale-Bopp*

It's gone now. The last glance I had was probably in July sometime, when it was no more than a misty dot in the northwestern sky, but even then I was awed by the rarity of what I was seeing: an honest to goodness comet, fuzzy tail and all.

The first time I saw it was a month or two before. I called inside the house for the family to come out and have a look, and the bunch of us stood on the lawn and stared. My youngest wasn't as impressed as my wife and I; after all, this is the electronic age, an era that Will Durant, were he to have recorded it, might have sardonically dubbed "the age of miracles". Today's children experience on a daily basis what my generation relegated to the domain of science fiction. For us, the arrival of television  was about as high as science could soar, or so we thought; but by the time I finished high school, radios could be bought that were no bigger than a pack of gum. Then came Sputnik and Apollo, Dien Bien Phu and Afghanistan, faxes and e-mails, and the list goes on.

The down side to the commonality of miracles is that today's children have been dispossessed of  the opportunity to be awed. Indeed, "awe" has yielded to its distant cousin "awesome", and in the process the aura of enigmatic reverence, a sense of being overwhelmed inherent in the root word, has all but disappeared. Music groups, a new boyfriend or girlfriend, clothing styles, Forest Gump, Michael Jordon: they're all "awesome", and the proliferating presence of the word has the effect of diluting its singularity with every use.

This isn't their fault though. They were born into it; their values and priorities are to a large measure a response to an instinct for survival, and, like it or not, we are their mentors. It is through watching and listening to us that these priorities are formed. By the same token, it will only be through our guidance that they will come to experience genuine awe.

Take that comet, for example. Perhaps it has a lot to do with my age and former profession but what was going through my mind as I stood on my lawn that night staring at the night sky wasn't science, astronomy, or even extraterrestrial life. No, my first thought was a quote from "Julius Caesar": "When beggars die there are no comets seen." Then I found myself wondering how many others in innumerable cities and villages around the world were at that very moment watching what I was watching.

That's when the truly "awesome" struck me. The last passing of what has in our decade been designated "Hale-Bopp" was over four thousand years ago. Three thousand seven hundred years before the arrival of Columbus; two thousand six hundred years before the fall of Rome; two millennia before the birth of Christ; eight hundred years before the reign of Tutankhamen. We in 1997 were witnessing what has been shrouded in the depth of space for most of the recorded history of humankind.

How might a clan of Red Clay Indians trading at the mouth of the Saint John River have greeted the spectacular apparition. A small community isolated by choice on the shores of an island at the mouth of a river, edged by a forest that extended intact for thousands of miles. A mountain of rock flanking the river's mouth and partially blocking the sky to the north. And there, high above, the blurred outline of a passing god or ancestor, either way an omen not to be ignored. Theirs was awe in its purest form: fear, amazement, reverence; overwhelming submissiveness.

There are those who would prefer words like ignorance, naivety, perhaps even savagery as more fitting. My place isn't to argue with them. Their world is their world; their miracles ones of their own choosing. As for me, I more easily identify with John Gillesipe Magee's ageless abstraction of what drew him to be a pioneer in the infancy of flight: "And while with silent, lifting mind I've trod the high untrespassed sanctity of space, put out my hand and touched the face of God."

    May all children, at least once in this twinkle we call a lifetime, find a moment to experience the same.

*Chopping Onions*

# *Officer Jack*

*"From Ghoulies And Ghosties And Long-Leggety Beasties*
*And Things That Go Bump In The Night,*
*Good Lord, Deliver Us"*

...Cornish Prayer

It isn't every college freshman who could brag of having met the man who outdrew Hoot Gibson. I realized this right away and was colossally impressed. After all, Hoot's quick draw was legendary, right up there with Tom Mix and Hoppy Cassidy. Apparently, though, he was no match for Officer Jack, sole member of the campus police force at Saint Francis Xavier, Antigonish, Nova Scotia.

I remember vividly the evening in the autumn of 1960 when Jack unfolded the anecdote to me. At the time I had a habit of walking over to the lounge area beneath the dining hall, the only spot left with a few bulbs burning after lights out, to catch up on my studies. Jack would usually happen by somewhere around ten or eleven o'clock and always brought with him a tall tale or two, ripe for the telling.

I have to admit it was a great story: Hoot visiting Antigonish, Hoot getting a little frisky somewhere downtown, Jack seeing it as an inescapable trust to settle things down. As he told it, they talked things over, just like Gary Cooper did before the bell tolled in High Noon, and came to a gentlemen's agreement: the slower draw would go home quietly. Need I go any farther? Suffice it to say that the lesser man lost that memorable night, and humility once again triumphed over pomposity.

I tell this story to give you a sense of how desperate university students in the early sixties, at least the ones in

Antigonish, were for a diversion. There wasn't a lot to do when one got bored with the books. I recall the highlight of many an evening being a brisk walk downtown where we'd gather in bunches of six or seven to watch the town's only baloney slicer. So it was that an opportunity to be regaled with one of Jack's harmless fantasies was as welcome as towels in a sauna.

Trouble was, we couldn't always rely on Jack to keep our imaginations warm. The safest thing was to find a kindred spirit or two and make up your own fun, provided of course no innocent bystander was compromised in the process.

That's how I came to meet Vince Walsh, a lanky guitar player from Worcester, Mass. whose inventiveness was without limit. Vince went home to stay at the end of his sophomore year, but in his wake he left enough harmless fun to fill a lifetime. Only once can I remember it getting us into some kind of trouble.

It was Halloween, 1961. Vince and I were walking from the downtown area in late afternoon when we met a few local goblins trying to get an early start.

"Not much in the line of costumes", Vince observed.

"Hardware store stuff. Garbage bags and lipstick. Kids today don't have the imagination we used to have."

So philosophical an observation was cause for pause, and we spent the next five or ten yards in private recollection of Halloweens gone by. Then Vince broke the silence.

"You know, I bet we could put together a dandy costume if we set our minds to it, something really ugly that'd shake this place up real good. What you think; worth a try?"

Twenty minutes later we were in Webb's Hardware Store picking among the rubber masks. We settled on a gnarled, aged oriental face with an enormous nose and long pony tail with a bow at the end. Then back to Vince's room where we dug up a pair of fur-lined winter gloves which we turned inside out so the furry stuff was on the outside. To the end of each finger we pasted pieces of stiff paper, long and curly like those pictures of Howard Hughes's nails when he finally went off the deep end. A flashlight was tucked securely into a pocket of Vince's long, navy trench coat and a thick scarf tied around his neck like a noose. We were ready for the acid test.

Each residence was connected to its neighbour by a basement passageway. As with the rooms upstairs, the two or three swinging bulbs that lit the passage were turned out at precisely eleven.

At ten fifty-five Vince took his position in a broom closet at the foot of the stairs and waited. Meanwhile I hid in a trunk room about half way along the hall where I could see (or at least hear) everything.

We didn't have long to wait. A minute or two after lights out we heard the door at the top of the stairs open and then close, followed by the hollow `pat... pat... pat' of hands feeling their way along the wall. Vince stayed perfectly still until the 'pat' was only a foot or so away. Then, with no warning whatsoever, he held the light chest high and aimed it at his chin. When he turned it on, even I jumped with surprise at what we'd created. There was a horrible scream, and then the victim sped by the room where I was standing, threading four or five trunks without touching one of them, laughing uncontrollably all the way.

Our original plan had been to end it all right there but this was too good to die just yet. Upstairs we went, to the room of a guy we mutually disliked. His roomy was still up, but the mark was sleeping soundly when we got there. Vince softly stroked his face with a furry hand until one eye opened in a semi-conscious haze. He wasn't semi-conscious for long though. In one slick move he was out of bed, on his feet, into the hall and down the stairs. The last we saw of him he was heading for the lounge under the dining hall, looking for Officer Jack no doubt.

It was getting late, but there was one more stop to make: the freshman residence. I went in by myself and headed for the upstairs hall where one light was usually left on. As expected there were a half dozen guys sitting around under the lone bulb.

"Did you hear?"

"Hear what?"

"About the ghost? It's back! Been seen in a dozen places in the last hour!"

"What ghost?"

They were hooked.

"Ghost of that football player who hanged himself Halloween night ten or twenty years ago because he didn't make the team. He's showed up in Mockler Hall, and Augustine, and down town, and ..."

I tried as hard as I could to look terrified as I glanced out the window at the end of the hall.

"There it is! Look?" I pointed toward the football field where Vince, his silhouette outlined by residence entrance lights, came wandering out of the shadows at the far goal line as per plan, dragging his right foot in the softness of the early snow as he headed for the opposite end zone.

"Look! See for yourself!"

It would have been the perfect ending to a perfect Halloween except for what happened next. Out of the same corner of the field from where Vince had ventured, only twenty or thirty yards behind, came Officer Jack. By this time he'd got word of the ghoulish figure that had accosted at least two people already that night, and he was going to make sure it didn't accost three. Something was quite odd about his pursuit though. Spry as he was, the gap between himself and Vince didn't close, almost as if he wasn't really certain he wanted to catch up.

When Vince realized he was being tailed, he headed for the nearest darkness and disappeared from our view around the corner of the chapel. So did Jack, about fifteen seconds later. As soon as he could, Vince got rid of the costume and headed for my room where we'd planned to meet and review the evening anyway. Needless to say we locked the door, ready to convince anyone who might happen by that Vince hadn't left the residence that evening.

The next night I was back in the lounge playing my weekly game of `catch up' when Jack dropped by as usual. He had a cup of coffee in his hand, usually a sign that he was ready for a long stay.

"Ever tell you about the time I came face to face with a real ghost?", he began.

As it turned out, Jack wasn't to have a lot of years left patrolling the sidewalks and hallways of Saint F. X., but he remained a favoured character for thousands of students who shared late hours with him in the dining hall lounge. His encounter with Vince that Halloween, recounted as only Jack could tell it, was to become one of his personal-favourite anecdotes.

Mine too, I must admit.

*Chopping Onions*

# *Summer Job*

When I came home for Easter holidays in my first year at university, my father in his own gentle way informed me that it was time to put out the feelers for a job. "You're not thinking of taking another summer off, are you?" Start looking now, he told me, and you'll have a better chance of getting something when you come back in May. So start looking I did. Not really hard, mind you; just a kind of a medium look, more a marginal glance than a good, solid search.

First off, I went to the post office because I was pretty sure any positions available would go to sons and daughters of postal employees anyway. Then Saint Joseph's and the General, carefully noting in my interview how difficult it was for me to look at blood, though, I assured them, I was comfortable I'd be able to get over it with a little practice. I even went through the motions of applying for a position with the city as a tour host but a few of the answers I put down in the "local history" quiz left me confident I wouldn't be getting a call from them. When nothing had materialized by late May I was secure this would be another summer at the beach. What I didn't count on, however, was my mother.

Mom knew everyone. From the Mayor to the Bishop to the guy who sliced the ham at Dominion Stores, she knew them all. The fact that her eldest had been so rudely snubbed in his quest for employment was tantamount to a personal insult, one she decided she'd remedy immediately. Two phone calls later I had an appointment for the following morning at Bathurst Containers on the West Side ( `Fairville', Mom always called it).

"Do you want me to go with you?"

"No, Mom, I'll be fine."

"You sure, now? I know them all, you know. I went to

school with Fred Roderick. Are you sure you don't want me to come with you?"

"No, Mom, thanks anyway but I'll be just great."

I had this picture of my mother, Fred Roderick and a dozen school friends seated in a classroom while Mom lectured on my qualifications for plant manager. And there'd be a test right afterwards.

"No, Mom; honest, I'll be fine by myself.'

So it was that the next morning I presented myself at the old Wilson Box Mill, now Bathurst Containers. There was no office to speak of, just a glassed-in observation tower in the center of the plant. I was handed one of those generic, pale green application forms, given a pen and gently pushed toward an armless chair to the right of the door. I'd already given some thought to what discouraging information I might offer but all my planning was for naught. "You Angie's boy?" He'd come up the stairs and entered the tower while my head was down. There was no name-tag but his shirt and tie told me he must be someone important, management probably. "You Angie's boy?", he repeated as if he hadn't heard himself the first time.

"Yes, Sir." I wasn't totally sure we were talking about the same Angie but given this was Fairville the likelihood of embarrassment was minuscule.

"Now which one are you: Fred or Jim?".

"Fred. Jim's the ugly one." My hesitant attempt at humour must have fallen on deaf ears because he continued as if I hadn't even answered.

"So you're looking for work, are you? Can you begin today?'

"Well, no sir, I still have to finish my term, and ..."

"Not a problem. When you through? May? May's perfect. Give us a call when you get back in May. Right?"

"Sure, sir. Thanks. May it is then."

When I finally arrived back in Saint John the third week in April, I avoided the topic of work in general and Bathurst

Containers in particular. Maybe, I said to myself, if I don't bring it up, Mom and Dad will let it fade gracefully. No such luck. The Friday before the first Monday in May, the phone rang.

"It's for you, dear", Mom called from the other room. Her "you-owe-me-big-time-and-aren't-you-impressed-with-your-mother's-efficiency" tone left me no doubt: it had to be Bathurst Containers.

The next morning when I presented myself at the time-clock, I was beginning to feel isolated, the new kid on the block, so to speak. Luck was on my side though. I spied a familiar face in the crowd: big Joe Flynn, a guy I clearly remembered from my South End Little League days. My luck doubled when I was assigned to work in the shipping department where, as it turned out, Joe was assistant shipper. Thus began a summer that wasn't quite as good as a beach but as close to it as the work world might allow. I was put on a special shift, ten in the morning until seven at night, loading trucks and doing odd jobs around the loading bays. I had my mornings to sleep in and lots of daylight left when it was time to go home. The summer flew by without any pain at all... a total waste because I learned nothing.

Things changed dramatically the following summer though. Getting back on with Bathurst wasn't the problem; no, the difficulty was the new work I was assigned: the printers. Here was genuine work, the kind that cut your hands, strained your back and left ugly gobs of ink under your nails. At the end of the day I was bona fide exhausted, wiped out, void of social ambition. And things only got worse. That summer, the Bathurst Container plants along the Saint Lawrence all went on strike and where do you suppose they channelled the work that normally would have gone to them? You guessed it, Saint John. For over a month we were put on twelve hour shifts, eight until eight, alternating each week. It was the toughest thing I'd yet had to face in my young life. I came close to quitting.

That's where Paddy enters the picture. His name was

Paddy McMullin and he was in charge of the printer where I worked. He and I were its crew, with Paddy the head guy. When first we met I must admit I was a little afraid of him. He seemed too quiet, almost surly, but that changed very quickly. He took me under his wing, tolerated me even, and patiently taught me what I was to do and how to do it. He had a really dry sense of humour which seemed to meld well with my admittedly off beat nature. Before long we became friends. Not the beer-drinking, hardy-har-har variety; just two people who seemed to understand and respect where each other was coming from.

One particularly long night we were taking our 2 a.m. break. Paddy and I were sipping coffee in the lunch room when exhaustion made me bare my soul.

"I don't think I can last it, Paddy. I guess I wasn't cut out for this sort of thing. Maybe I should quit while I'm still half alive."

He stirred his coffee by moving it around in tiny circles on the table in front of him.

"Don't like this kinda work?"

"Not in the slightest. Last summer wasn't bad; but this one, well..." I rolled my eyes to make my point.

"That's where you're lucky. You won't hav'ta do this all your life. Remember when you go back to school, this is why you're there. Think about it and you'll see what I mean."

I did think about it. And I did see what he meant. And more than that, I appreciated the wisdom he was sharing with me: the greater the education, the less likely it will be you'll spend your life doing something you really don't want to do.

That evening Paddy became somewhat of a hero in my young eyes. And that summer, very much the "summer of my discontent" (apologies to John Stienbeck), I learned what had escaped me the summer before.

I've always regretted that I never took the time to tell this to Paddy.

Thanks, my friend. Now I feel better.

# *Gerry Lynch*

My father was a man who loved sport from a distance. This grew as much out of necessity as of anything else; his job as a barber, the same job that negated the time to take in a hockey or baseball game, required that he be knowledgeable, indeed somewhat of an expert, on those common sports that inevitably surface in that conversation associated with an average haircut. Along the way, in keeping up with who "won" and who was second, he came to appreciate and admire some of our cities "really great ones".

As a youngster waiting in a corner of the barber shop to walk him home on a Saturday afternoon, I'd listen in amazement to stories both fanciful and real. Soon I was making mental note of those athletes whom my father seemed genuinely to admire and without ever having met them they became my heroes too.

Gerry Lynch was one of these.

When first I did meet Gerry, I had no idea who he was. It was more than thirty years ago and he was umpiring softball when our Knights of Columbus team played in a fun league once or twice a week. Long before I found out he was the Gerry Lynch my father used to tell me about, I was already struck with how friendly a person he was. He never raised his voice or lost his temper or in any way gave us a hint of how truly pathetic we sometimes were. He'd congratulate us when we did well, say nothing when we didn't and then slip quietly into the sunset when the game was over, like a Zorro or a Lone Ranger. When I did find who he was, I was awe-struck. He was the first of my father's heroes that I'd met in the flesh and as such, though Gerry would have had no way of knowing it, he had a difficult image to live up to.

But "live up" to it he did. As time went on and as I became more aware of his amazing success on hockey rink and baseball diamond, I also came to know and respect him on other, totally different levels. I discovered and admired him as a father when I met his sons, as a husband when he spoke of his wife, and in later years as a man of deep faith when our paths crossed every Sunday at the Cathedral.

Ironically, it was the Gerry of the Cathedral that I'll most remember. For years he was one of a group of gentlemen who'd collect the offering at the 11:30 mass on Sunday. He'd always be there early, sitting in the back pew beside the glass partition by the main door. On days when my family and I used that entrance, he'd mouth a "hi" from ten or so feet away and give a slightly perceptible, chest-high wave so as to avoid bothering those around him. More than likely, however, because we'd most often park to the side of the church and enter from that door, I wouldn't see Gerry until collection time, provided he was assigned to our corner of the congregation. If so, the big smile would light up a couple of pews away and an audible "How's she goin', Fred" would be the greeting. On Sundays when he harvested at some other aisle, I'd kneel patiently after communion until Gerry worked forward from his accustomed place at the end of the line. Then he'd touch my shoulder to get my attention, shake my hand, offer another big smile and a "How's she goin', Fred" and move on.

Early this year, things began to change. Gerry took to missing the occasional Sunday, and at those masses when he *was* there he'd sometimes sit quietly in his seat while others took up the offering. Such Sundays became more and more frequent, and I soon came to realise how much that touch on the shoulder and the "How's she goin', Fred" had become a part of my Sunday experience. Silly as it might sound, Gerry's absence meant something was missing, something at once real and metaphorical.

That's when a mutual friend told me how sick Gerry was. I made it a point of calling him that week and was encouraged by the strength in the voice that answered me. As we talked, my mind drifted to my standing in the window of my parents apartment overlooking University Avenue, and my father pointing out Gerry and his dog as they were out for their evening stroll.

Gerry was buried yesterday from the Cathedral that he loved. On those few Sundays since July when he'd been strong enough to come back, I'd always made it a point to shake his hand and make him feel welcome. We'd talk for a few minutes until I couldn't ignore the line-up of other friends who wanted to say hello and then I'd move on, but before we parted, I always made a special effort to touch my hand to his shoulder for just a second.

I'd like to think he knew exactly what I was saying.

# *Soda Fountains I Have Known*

Growing up in the fifties wasn't as effortless as "Happy Days" re-runs might suggest; not for me anyway. Apart from C.Y. Hi dances (to attend a dance at the YMCA was to risk Excommunication), any social confidence I managed to harvest was sown at one of the many uptown soda fountains either after school or on weekends. No doubt about it; if it weren't for those flavoured cokes I might not have survived.

I have no idea when the Kosy Korner first opened but I'm pretty sure it was soon after the new Saint Malachy's High opened in the Fall of 1954. It was, as its name punfully implies, a cosy little spot with a soda counter and a dozen or so booths perfect for those cliquish get togethers that proclaimed the edge of the city you called home. The place probably had a menu of sorts but most of our spending was devoted to the fad of the day, cokes with a swish of artificial flavouring: vanilla, cherry, strawberry and so on. Vanilla was my personal favourite with cherry probably a close second. With practice, a normal-sized glass could last for upwards of an hour if we weren't too thirsty and didn't rush it. Our limited pockets never seemed to concern the proprietors. Quite to the contrary really; they made us feel genuinely welcome provided we didn't get so loud as to scare away the real paying customers with their hot hamburgs, fries and gravy.

An added bonus to the Kosy was its proximity to Kings Square, the nerve center of what was then uptown Saint John. Every bus worth its salt eventually made its way directly (or via a transfer) to the Square, which made it possible to nurse that coke for a good hour and still be home in time for supper. The drivers understood; they'd be the last to admit it but they always snuck a

103

final peek toward the bandstand for stragglers before beginning their five o'clock runs.

Each booth had its own miny juke box with accompanying offering of fifty or sixty current finger-snappers at a nickel a pop, six for a quarter. And the tables were the perfect size to accommodate three or four notebooks and an Algebra text, provided there was a math whiz in the group. Homework was never easier than to the accompaniment of Connie Francis and a sip of vanilla coke.

Down the hill at the corner of Prince Edward and Union was The Hobby Shop. Early on, maybe up until `55 or so, it had been just what the name implies: a glorious celebration of every plane, boat or car kit there was to offer. When it eventually became clear to the proprietors that model kits couldn't sustain the place without some additional variety, they added a few amply stocked shelves of juvenile-style novels and finally a soda counter and half-dozen booths. This was another favourite place, to a large part because of Clyde Carter, the young guy not a lot older than we were who worked there and who went out of his way to make us feel welcome. When the store wasn't too busy he'd join us in a booth or at the counter and talk hockey, baseball or school sports: whatever we had on our mind. I especially remember the Saturday morning he proudly announced he was going to be a policeman and how much he was looking forward to the challenge. Years later, when I would be sitting talking to my father in his barbershop at Haymarket Square, Clyde would often take a few minutes from his beat to talk his newest passion with us: scuba diving. I admired him very much but, as time often has it, never got the chance to tell him so. He drowned doing what he loved.

And there was the Riviera Restaurant, and Walsh's Drugstore on Prince Edward at Haymarket, and Woolworth's and Driscoll Drugs on Union, and many others that escape me at the moment: each at once universal yet unique; harmless places where many a youthful wing was first spread.

My unquestionable favourite though was Moore's Drug

Store. It sat beside the old Music Conservatory at the corner of Richmond and Prince Edward, only a five minute walk from where I lived on Exmouth, the perfect distance for justifying a thirty minute hiatus from an evening's homework. Two or three nights a week at precisely eight thirty, the books would be put away long enough to wander down and say hello to Tm Isaac who delivered prescriptions part-time and, if my memory doesn't fail me, could be reasonably generous with the vanilla flavouring. The atmosphere of the place was perfect: rows of magazines, glassed cases sheltering colourful odds and ends in every colour imaginable, candies and cough drops, pens and pencils and that ever present clock on the wall that reminded us when we'd been there long enough.

They're all gone now. Not the buildings, mind you. With the exception of Walsh's which gave way to urban renewal and The Riv, claimed by fire, what's left of them still stands. But Tim tells me what very well could be the last genuine soda counter in the city was removed recently from a store near him on Prince William Street; shipped to Saint Andrews it was, hopefully to someone who'll appreciate the stories it could tell.

*Chopping Onions*

# *Charlie O'Hara*

For a young man who'd never been away from home much more than a weekend and even then no farther than Dipper Harbour, my first train ride to Antigonish and Saint Francis Xavier in September of 1960 was a traumatic one. Worse than actually leaving was the anticipation of leaving, and as August stepped aside for September and my younger brother went back to school for his grade 10 year, I was having second thoughts, the kind that visit late at night when everyone else is sleeping and you're left alone with secret misgivings.

My mother had begun preparations in early July. In retrospect I now realize it was just her way of tabling our approaching severing of the umbilical cord, so to speak. She set about sewing my name on everything wearable, hoarding toiletries and neatly packing it all, piece by piece, in an enormous blue trunk purchased at MRA's. Two days before I was scheduled to leave, a big truck arrived at the door to transport it to the Union Station in the hope that the trunk might reach Antigonish before I did. When that trunk left, I secretly accepted what I'd known all along: it was too late now to change my mind.

Up until this time my only experiences with Union Station, other than flashes from my childhood, were those Saturday or Sunday afternoons when my friends and I would walk back from St. Peter's Park after watching a ball game. It struck me then as a cold, cavernous place which for some reason or other I associated with sadness. It never crossed my mind that people, real people, worked there on a daily basis and that some of them went out of their way to make coming home a happy thing and parting a sweeter sorrow than might normally be expected. Over the next four years I would learn that lesson well.

Stepping into the station was like entering an enormous mausoleum. At floor level were news kiosks, a snack shop, an alcove of telephones and parallel rows of deacon's benches arranged to face the exit in the northeast corner that led to the platforms and the waiting trains. That's where I first met Charlie O'Hara, though I wouldn't know him by name until my second or third trip.

My first impression was his broad smile, a smile slightly wider than he was tall. Like Peter at the gate, he ushered each of us through the portals with a genuine pat on the shoulder and friendly reminder of the track appropriate to our Moncton train. What I remember is that he greeted me with friendly respect rather than the condescending stiffness I'd previously associated with so many adults in positions of authority. When it came time for the train to leave, there was Charlie again, standing with the parents and waving to anyone who might wave back.

That October when I came home for Thanksgiving, he was waiting at the station door, the first person to meet and greet. So too on Remembrance Day, Christmas and Spring break. In time, I came to associate Charlie O'Hara with coming home, and Union Station with Charlie O'Hara. By the beginning of my sophomore year we were on a first name basis and when finally I did come home to stay, I made a special trip to Station Street to thank him for having always being there.

That didn't end my association with Charlie. When I began my teaching career in the mid-sixties, his daughter Colleen was in my class. Over the next three decades, Charlie would keeping popping up when least expected, like a Leprechaun in a field of shamrocks. He never seemed to get older and always sported that foot-wide smile as soon as he recognized me. I quickly came to realize how well-known and popular a gentleman he was. Everyone knew and respected him for reasons no more complicated than his being a genuinely nice person who couldn't for the life of him control an unconditional love of uncomplicated conversation. Wherever and whenever you might cross his path, he was ready and willing to chat.

As the years passed, he might have slowed down a bit and got a little unsteady on his feet but his zest for life never faded in the least. It seemed infinitely appropriate to me, and more than a little poetic, when students responsible for the Union Station mural across from Harbour Station chose to include a depiction of Charlie to complete their effort. In my eyes, after all, the building owed whatever life it might have had to him and to people like him. The east-west railroad line has long since been succeeded by a modern highway and the stones that were Union Station reduced to decorating the walls of a bank, but thanks to the Charlie O'Haras of the our city most of us remember anyway.

Charlie left us last Friday. Personally, I'd like to think of his passing as a promotion of sorts, from one gate to another you might say. Move over, Peter. There's a little guy with an enormous smile on his way to give you a hand.

*Chopping Onions*

# *Murphy's Law:*

## *"If Anything Can Go Wrong, It Will"*

...Anonymous

I've always had an affinity for the Halifax area, especially the area around Lower Sackville and Bedford. That's where Frank and Winnie lived, and they always made me feel welcome.

When I left Saint John to attend university in Antigonish it was the first time I'd been away from home for any length of time. Mind you, I liked Saint Francis Xavier and Antigonish in general, but the absence of familiar faces other than the few high school friends who'd caught the eastbound with me made the first few months a little empty. That's where Frank and Winnie enter the picture.

Winnie was my father's sister and a favourite aunt. Frank was technically my uncle, but he was such a pleasant person to be with that he'd surpassed the uncle-nephew thing to become what I considered a genuinely nice guy and a pretty close friend. While I lived in Saint John I'd only see them once a year when they'd spend a week or so at the family homestead on the Churchland Road. Their oldest girl, Maureen, and her brother Terry were about my age so we got to know each other better and better as each summer passed. A second daughter, Helen, was closer to my brother than to me, and the "baby" (she'd shoot me if she ever heard I called her that), Kathy, seldom let herself get separated from the end of her mom's skirt.

Anyway, I guess my letters home gave my parents a pretty good barometer of the separation anxiety I was weathering because I received a note one October afternoon from Aunt Winnie inviting me to drop by some weekend. The timing of the invitation was perfect. That's when Saint F. X. was a football powerhouse, and the

Purdy Cup, held every November at Wanderer's Grounds in Halifax, was only two weeks away. Seeing Maureen and Terry again would be a nice break too. That was the first of my many visits to Lower Sackville in the early sixties. They were great times, warm, fun times, from which I'll always cherish special memories.

At the end of my first year of teaching I had this great idea to have a bit of a nostalgia trip. I'd drive to Antigonish, then on to the Cabot Trail, and from there over to Halifax to see Frank and Winnie and their brood. I talked Bill Harkins and Jim Hope into joining me, bragging wildly about the scenery, the weather, the hospitality and anything else I could think of to coax them along. It didn't take much coaxing, though. Jim had just finished his stint in the air force and Bill, a teacher himself and a self-proclaimed history nut, was ready and willing for anything that smelled of adventure.

Our transportation was to be my father's aging '61 Dodge Pioneer, an enormous but aerodynamically pleasing vehicle with a grotesquely wide rear deck. Driving behind it must have been akin to tailing Moby Dick. It was a two-door hardtop which in its day had been quite the wagon but by then it had already begun to squeak and sputter where squeaks and sputters had no right to be.

The first part of the trip was uneventful: Antigonish, Cape Breton, Antigonish again, and then on to Halifax. Unfortunately, Frank and Winnie and the family were out of town but they'd generously left us with the house as long as we wanted it. The only down side to the arrangement was their border, a barber who worked just up the road and who spoke very little English and lots of something else I couldn't put a label on. We kept our distance though, and the covenant worked well for the first two days.

On the evening of the second day, the three of us brought a pizza home from the mall and settled down for a quick meal. After a few bites into our first pieces, a short and somewhat muffled toot of a car horn caught our attention. Jim, sitting near the kitchen window, glanced outside but no one was around. A minute or so later we heard it again, more insistent this time, but still the street outside was deserted. I figured it was just some teens who'd taken a shine to Maureen or Helen and who, unaware they weren't home, were trying to get their attention. When the horn blew for about the tenth time, though, we decided enough was enough. Out the back door we went, ready to send the little hooligans on their way.

That's when Jim noticed something quite odd. The Pioneer was parked in the corner of the yard, its headlights blinking as if someone were inside playing with the switch.

"They're tryin' to steal the car!"

Jim's military training kicked in automatically. Down the steps he ran, grabbing a broom at the foot of the stairs along the way. In quieter moments since, I've often wondered what he would have done with the broom if thieves had actually been there, but that wasn't the case. It was about three feet from the car that we got our second clue: the acrid smell of rubber burning. That, coupled with the smoke that was by now curling from beneath the hood, gave us our answer: the car was on fire!

What followed was a textbook study in panic. I immediately went to the trunk, unlocked it calmly, and took out a big paint brush my father had left there. Then I closed the trunk, taking care to be sure the latch had caught, and stood there with a paint brush in my hand, looking a lot like the Statue of Liberty. Bill meanwhile had adopted a wait and see, "let's look this thing over carefully" reaction. Through the growing haze of the smoke I could see him near the driver's door, one hand in his pocket and the other fingering the collar of his shirt. Clearly he had the situation well in hand.

Jim was the only one with any sense. It was he who, realizing that what we had here was one of your everyday variety electrical fires, threw open the hood and brutalized the battery with his broomstick, finally prying loose one of the cables. The horn was finally silent.

For the next three days, while the local Dodge dealer was installing a new wire harness, we came to loathe each other. No, there were no fisticuffs or anything like that, but with nothing to do but play cribbage from dawn till dusk, keeping one's cool was a bit of a problem. And the unilingual border was no help either. He even complained one evening that we were moving the pegs too loudly. After that we kept score with a hammer and a box of nails.

Finally we got a call informing us the car was ready. The dealer apologized that it'd taken so long but explained that no one in the shop had ever done a job like this before and they'd had to feel their way along, but they were pretty sure everything was okay now. We accepted the apology, paid the bill, and got out of there faster than you could say "mad unilingual person who cuts hair".

The way home was much more relaxing; well, most of the way anyway.

Right up to when I pushed in the cigarette lighter and the radio came on!

It took me a good ten minutes to find how to turn on the lights.

# *Quinn's Pond*

To the best of my knowledge, Quinn's Pond doesn't exist anymore. Even if's still sitting there I'd really prefer to keep my distance. Too much of my youth and young adulthood are laid to rest in its mossy hollows.

Thirty or forty years ago, the way to get there was a little more complicated than it is today. A drive up the Churchland Road from Dolan's Lake, then a left onto a very narrow Sproul Road until we'd almost reached the base of Ben Lomond Mountain; from there, a walk down an English-style country lane like the ones that still pop up every so often on PBS, alder canopied and the greenest of greens. On those mornings when we choose to stick to the lane the reward was a small, horse-shoe-shaped lake we called Minote. Others called it Harrisons' Lake because of the summer home Judge Harrison kept on its shores for many years, but my father's family called it Minote so I did too.

Quinn's Pond wasn't quite as accessible though. First there was a sharp-eyed search for that slightest hint of a brook, maybe a foot across at its widest point, flowing serendipitously down an abrupt embankment concealed by tall softwoods and carpets of ferns. In some spots we had to bend low to worm our way under the lower bows and protect our eyes from the stinging slap of spruce and fir needles, not an easy task when walking downhill while carrying a fishing rod and a can of worms. Then, as suddenly as the ground levelled, the forest opened into a scene more peaceful than ever captured by camera or brush.

An almost circular little pool, glass smooth in the shelter of the arboreal bowl that surrounded it. Not so much as the slightest ripple to sully the mirror that was its surface. On one side was a sandy shore of perhaps fifteen feet, but most of its perimeter was densely overgrown, leaving only two or three decent spots from which a line could be cast. The fish weren't very big, just pan-sized at best, much like up the hill in Minote, but sweet tasting and with more colour than a box of crayolas.

When it was sunny, the taller trees shaded Quinn's for most of the day, keeping it fresh and cool, and when it rained, all that reached us was the steady but soft droplets falling from the foliage overhead. A hour or two at poolside could almost guarantee the visit of a few squirrels, a rabbit or the occasional partridge, but rare were the days when another of our species would happen by for any more than a short visit. Only a lucky few knew of Quinn's, locals or sons and daughters of locals, and they were most respectful of the solemnity of the setting. One visitor was perfect, and two was acceptable provided they were good friends appreciative of the serenity of silence. But two strangers, or even two casual acquaintances, was one too many. Beauty was made to be shared, but not if it has to be diluted.

One particular visit always comes to mind when I think of Quinn's. It was my very first time into the hollow and I was in my early teens. I'd had a disappointingly unproductive morning at the mouth of Dolan's Lake and my father had asked if I wanted to try a new spot. This led to a quick drive up the road where we parked on the soft shoulder of the Sproul and made our way to Minote and down to the pond. Dad had things to do around the camp so he made sure I knew where I was and then headed back to Dolan's. When evening came I was getting ready to head out to the road where I knew he'd be waiting for me when out of the corner of my eye I caught a quick movement in the deepening darkness. A small trout had playfully broken the surface of the water, leaving in its wake an increasing series of concentric circles moving outward toward the pool's edge. That's when I saw the most magnificent of images in the water's surface. Thousands of stars and a brilliant moon mirroring the heavens directly above. A universe captured in a tiny pond no bigger than a heartbeat. But it was late and, as Frost so aptly put it, I had promises to keep. So I left, and the moment ended.

My last brief visit to Quinn's Pond was perhaps twenty years ago. It was very much as it had been on that afternoon of my first visit, but with one ominous addition. Survey markers ran along a freshly cut path that crossed the Sproul within a stone's throw of the entrance to Minote. In a few years, heavy equipment moved in and within a decade a new highway was built. Appropriately, the Sproul Road was renamed the Cozy Lake Road; I say "appropriately" because in my eyes and in the eyes of many others it wasn't the Sproul that we'd known and loved. Cars and trucks now cross the very spots where deer had grazed and apples had grown wild and sweet.

I stopped at the top of the rise and stared into the hollow below, but I went no farther. I'd made the mistake before of "going back", and had learned my lesson the hard way. Today, despite the reality that is unavoidable every time I drive in the direction of the airport, I still have one treasure that is mine alone, securely tucked in a fold of memory.

A universe captured in a tiny pond no bigger than a heartbeat.

*Chopping Onions*

# *Remember Radio?*

Back when we were struggling through grade school and into our early teens, television was not yet the `big thing' it is today. We relied on radio for everything that really mattered: information, music, comedy, and more drama than most of us could handle.

One of my earliest memories (honest!) is of the family literally seated around the radio listening to different favourite programs every day of the week. Some of the shows were group favourites: Fibber Magee and Molly, Amos and Andy, Jack Benny. Others were more for the kids, like The Lone Ranger ("Out of the west comes the pound of hoof beats..."), The Shadow ("What evil lurks in the heart of man? The Shadow knows!"), and the original Bergen, Edgar, with his sidekicks, Charlie and Mortimer. Then there was those live World Series games (I heard Willie Mays make that catch in the `54 Series two weeks before I actually saw it, and when I did get to see it I was only 75% satisfied), the Stanley Cup, and an occasional all-star game.

What made radio really great was its dramatic effectiveness. The listening was only the beginning of the experience; after that, the imagination would kick in and we'd add the visual and tactile effects totally on our own. Sure, I knew what Silver or Champion or Trigger sounded like (amazingly similar to coconut shells banging together), but I also knew what they looked like. I could feel the leather of the saddle, the bounce of a gallop, and yes, every now and then I even caught a whiff of barn floor (though I can't remember Hoppy or Lone ever commenting).

The problem was that when television finally did come along, all my seeing was done for me, and I must admit that

many times I wasn't totally happy with the experience. Gene Autry looked a little too wimpy for my liking, and I could have sworn Rocket Richard was a foot or so taller. Jay Silverheels made a great Tonto, and Eve Arden was a prettier Miss Brookes than I might have allowed, but I was destroyed when Roy Rogers started hanging around with a guy who drove a Jeep.

Things changed slowly though. Old habits are hard to discard. By the time high school rolled around, radio was still my most important study aid. I'd sit in a big chair beside a front window, doing Physics or Math or History to the beat of the

Everlys or Bobby Darin. And here's an "I-speak-the-truth" irony for you; for weeks I struggled over Archimedes Principle, night after night, and then one evening it hit me like an epiphany, right in the middle of "Splish, Splash"! I kid you not!

Radio helped me with my social life every now and then too. It was back when the invention of the transistor spawned those tiny machines with equally tiny earplugs that were great for anything within five or six miles but useless beyond that. They had little wires about a meter long that could be run up a wall or attached to a radiator to improve reception by a few feet or so. We used to gather in little globs of five or six teens, each armed with his or her tiny auditory unit, sitting by the edge of the lake and snapping our fingers in unison to some tune we could individually but not collectively hear.

That's when the guys and girls around the Grove made a big discovery. Back then, you might remember, telephone wires ran in pairs, with two or three pairs to a pole. These wires often came quite close to the ground, especially in the country where fairly substantial slopes characterized the sides of most roads, at least the Golden Grove Road anyway. Well, our discovery was that if we were to attach that tiny aerial wire to a telephone line, what we got was an aerial maybe two million miles long. Heck, on a good night we'd get all the great ones, KBW, WINS, the Wolf Man, and a mess of others that we could barely raise on our big sets back home. The bunch of us could spend an entire evening sitting on a rock under telephone wires and sharing earplugs whenever we discovered a new station. Admittedly it wasn't all that sanitary, but when you're young, romance comes in bits and pieces.

The gran'daddy of radios used to sit on a table beside the old sofa at our summer place. I think it was a Marconi, though I wouldn't swear to it, but I do remember it had a short wave band in addition to the normal stations. A spin dial on its face made it easy to locate even the most sensitive of stations, so a bunch of us would sit around well into the night surfing the dial like modern day couch potatos. That way we got to hear the latest songs long before local stations even received the records.

We got a head start on the news too. It was close to 2 AM one evening when I clearly remember picking up the news that Pius XII had died. I remember calling my mother and father (they were at our flat in the city) to tell them, but they wouldn't believe me. Neither did the local radio station when we called them too. Come morning, we waited for an apology that never came.

I mention the Pius XII recollection because its was the first of two radio moments that are as clear to me today as if they were just happening. In each case, I can remember where I was sitting, what I was wearing, even the way the conversation was going when the news hit. The difference between the two is that the other recollection came at a time in my life when I was a little more than a kid but not quite yet an adult. Maybe that's why it's so clear to me: here, now and for ever.

Sitting in the car in front of the Villa Madonna Retreat House... talking to a friend who is standing on the veranda... the sound of music coming from a radio just inside the door... laughing about the news that I'd decided to become a teacher... and the interruption itself, a sonorous voice that couldn't completely mask the horrified excitement of the broadcaster, telling us that someone had fired a shot at President Kennedy's motorcade. For the next week, the whole world watched and listened, but how were we to know that nothing would ever be the same again.

I still listen to radio now, but most of the time its while I'm driving to or from somewhere. Like old friends who pass on the street and engage in brief conversation, we share a moment or two and then get on with our lives.

# *Smith Cathline*

*"I think I don't regret a single excess' of my responsive youth.
I only regret, in my chilled age, certain occasions
and possibilities I didn't embrace."*

...Henry James

To the young people around Dolan's Lake, Smith Cathline was a special character. He was their only tie with the outside world, the high tech one boldly displayed on the backs of breakfast cereals and popsicle wrappers. For a ridiculously small investment (including postage) a lucky kid could be "the first on the block" to boast that flashy new jack-knife with everything but a blade, or an "authentic" rubber ball made from the same "durable" material as airplane tires. Just sign on the dotted line, send along that ridiculously small investment (including postage), and your heart's desire would be on its way "by return mail".

That's where Smith entered the picture. He was our rural mailman, responsible for a route that included Lower and Upper Golden Grove, the Churchland, and the French Village as far as Kallers Corner. Encapsulated in any of a number of pick-up trucks he drove over the years, he'd set out early each morning to deliver his bag of dreams, along with yesterday's paper, a few bills, and even the occasional registered letter.

That's how I came to meet him. I'd sent for one of those triple-coloured, multi-beamed, solid plastic flashlights like the one Flash Gordon carried in his utility belt. The back of the fudgesicle sleeve had warned I should wait three weeks for delivery, but the order had been sent in late March and now it was almost the end of July; and flashlights were no good after school started!

Everyone knew that!

Each morning I'd wait at the side of the road for Smith's Chev to come over the hill by the Osborne place. As soon as I saw him I'd wander very nonchalantly in the opposite direction, as if it just happened I was there at precisely that moment every morning; nothing whatsoever to do with my Flash flashlight. Still, Smith was always good about it. He'd take the time to look through every package, though I'm sure he knew mine wasn't there. Then he'd sooth the disappointment just a little by asking me how the trout were biting, or if I'd run across any good-size snakes lately.

One morning he surprised me. He asked would I like to come along for the drive, "lend a hand" with his deliveries. I checked with my mother, and ten minutes later we were on our way. I had no way of knowing it then, but this was the innocent beginning of a "Jake And The Kid" relationship which was to last until the summer I graduated from high school.

Smith lived on a small farm a short distance along the Frog Pond Road. He didn't have much livestock there, but he kept twenty or thirty head of cattle on a larger piece of acreage over on Darling's Island. In the morning he'd deliver his mail but the rest of the day he'd putter around the barn doing any of the thousand little jobs that go with living in the country.

He was a big man, well over six feet with a bulk to match. To this day I can still picture him lifting a stubborn calf over a fence or effortlessly carrying enormous bags of potatoes he occasionally sold from the back of his truck. He was a gentle giant who loved kids and respected everyone else.

By the time I'd reached grade eleven, Smith decided I was old enough to help with two or three weeks of haying, enough to keep the cattle until spring. It was an experience I still remember whenever I have to make a trip to the Parkway Mall. This was one of the two spots that were his to hay, the other one being just off the Frog Pond Road. The Parkway spot was behind his sisters house, more or less where the eastern end of the mall sits today. The place was very marshy, so much so that on more than one occasion our wagon (and later our rented truck) would slip into one of the many drainage ditches that thread the area. But the best part was the trip up and over the rise now Forest Hills but then little more than trees and grass. I'd lie by myself on top of the hay in the back of the wagon, staring straight up and bathing in the dusty bouquet of imminent autumn.

Back at the barn, it was my job to stay in the loft and distribute the bundles as the big rope-drawn fork lifted bunch after bunch through a narrow side window. The experience of a lifetime: the loft, perfumed with clover and timothy; swallows darting chaotically from rafter to window, caught up in the excitement of harvest; and coming home at the end of the day, totally exhausted but somehow at peace with the feeling that I was a part of something bigger than I could understand.

The four or five summers Smith and I shared were good for the both of us. He was always picking my brain for how I was reacting to front page stories each day. His probing made me start reading newspapers seriously, trying to anticipate whatever observation or question he might bring up. In turn I would rummage among the countless anecdotes about Golden Grove and its people, a people that included my father and his family and the families of many of my friends. I came to know each very well, details I could never have picked up in a text book. The gospel according to Smith: inciteful, human, sometimes funny, always moving.

The summer before I left for university was filled with those distractions that confuse the end of adolescence. Smith would still drop by to invite me along every now and then, but I was a big boy now, a soon-to-be college freshman, and the romance of those daily trips had lost a lot of its appeal. I think Smith picked up on this fairly quickly because after a week or two he'd pause to chat whenever he saw me but stopped inviting me along. "Stranger!", he'd salute me, and we'd visit for five or ten minutes. But I must admit I still enjoyed those little conversations. They were friendly, sometimes even confiding; pleasant reminders that my innocence wasn't gone just yet.

That September, when I left for Antigonish, I left more than Saint John behind. Had I been wise enough to listen, I might have caught the gentle whisper of receding youth, but such wisdom, it would seem, is reserved for middle age. I had no idea where I was going and very little appreciation of where I'd been.

Eight or nine months later, I met Smith outside the Woolworth store on Charlotte Street. At first I didn't recognize him, not even when he playfully elbowed me, but the familiar inflection in "Stranger!" was unmistakable. For only the second time in my life I stood face to face with death.

The other time I had been a five-year-old led uncomfortably into the funeral parlour where my grandmother was being waked. I didn't really understand what was happening but I could sense the seriousness of the situation in the stillness of the room, the oppressive odour of flowers and the gentle touch of my mother's hand on my shoulder.

This time though I didn't have a mother's love to lean on. I didn't know what to say. His appearance had altered tremendously. The Smith before me bore no resemblance to him of my youth. A grossly oversized windbreaker hanging from his emaciated frame exaggerated freakishly narrow shoulders and a crane-like neck layered in ashen folds of skin. His jaw, cheek-bones and nose jutted monstrously from what once had been a familiar face. But his eyes, it was his eyes most of all. Alert, piercing, the only part of him that at all resembled the man I had known. Imprisoned inside this attenuated body was a mind and soul: bright, alert, resigned.

That evening Dad noticed my silence and asked if there was something wrong. I lied. I told him I just had a bit of a cold, but the real truth was I couldn't erase the image of Smith shuffling uncomfortably as we both struggled for something to say, and of the betrayal I felt for deserting him when he most needed me. I made a mental note to call him during the weekend.

I didn't.

When I returned to school I resolved that I'd go see him when I came home again in a couple of months.

I couldn't.

Three weeks later he died.

# *It Don't Snow Like It Used To*

It snowed last night. Again!

I know that doesn't merit a ton of attention after a life time of eastern-Canadian winters, but this one just struck me a little differently. Maybe because it's only early December, and we've had precious few early December snows of any significance over the past decade and a half; or maybe because these are my first few winters of retirement, a condition I'm not altogether used to just yet, love it though I may.

The rest of the family were elated, especially son and daughter still in school. To them it was a day off, twenty-four hours of unsolicited freedom, a golden opportunity to be bored at home rather than somewhere else. For tire stores around town it was a Christmas bonus, just in time to fill that impossible quota the head office shackled them with. To closet poets

(and we've got plenty to brag about), it was "nature's downey white mantle", or "a marshmallow world" (choke, choke), or even, perish the image, "a cotton candy kingdom". Mr. Quinlan, my neighbour from across the street, dubbed it quite appropriately "an old fashioned winter". Had Walter Cronkite been here he might have more stoically dubbed it, "a day like all days, filled with those things that alter and illuminate our time". Easy enough for you to say, Wally; obviously you've never experienced the joy of two-foot drifts plugging a fifty foot driveway.

It was in this spirit, seven or eight years ago, that I first admitted encroaching old age and bought myself a snowblower. Not one of those little sissy ones that do more spitting than blowing; no, my choice was a muscular, ten horse-power growler that would double as a summer Harley if I took the time to do the customizing. Point that baby in the direction of a super-drift and hold on hard. And throw snow? You haven't seen snow throwin' until you see US throw snow! Many a low-flying bird has learned the hard way to soar high when the growler and I are at work.

So it was that I struggled into my storm woollies, dug out my custom-fit, down-filled snow gloves, zipped up my boots and headed for the garage where the growler spends his idle time. From the end of the driveway I surveyed the task at hand: an expanse of white stuff the length of the Saint Lawrence and half as wide. No problem for the growler and me though; we'd taken on a lot worse in our time. "Length of the Saint Lawrence" was our middle name. A half hour later it was all over but the sanding.

Then it was reward time: a half-hour drive to nowhere in particular, kind of a throw-back to when our rock-dwelling ancestors spent half a day lugging their most recent kill from cave to cave, partly to season the meat but mostly to establish a decent brag. I first discovered the joy of these little drives when we lived in a garageless apartment and had to shovel out the car twenty times a winter. After a good bout of snow-butt kicking there was something delicious about aimlessly meandering the neighbourhood, slowing down when passing other poor clods who hadn't yet finished their exhumations, and giving the horn an arrogant little nudge. Good snow tires were important though because you had to be ready to get out of there quickly. There was always one or two who missed the humour.

But no sooner had I backed out of our driveway when I had this sudden flashback to winters a half century ago, the ones we talk about when snow piles were three times taller than we were, when traffic was light enough we could sled in the middle of the street,  when heading for school that morning was an adventure. Those were the days of "one sessions", when yellow busses were relegated to country roads and most of us walked to our neighbourhood school, all the while hoping beyond hope we'd be free by noon hour. Then home again to spend the remaining four or five hours of daylight playing King Of The Castle on the biggest snow pile we could find. In those days we might see a city snow-blower once a winter if at all, and even then it was usually late February or even March, a sure sign of Spring. Plow after plow, storm after storm, the snow accumulated, eventually creating enormous mounds many feet thick and three times as high, perfect for climbing and tunnelling.

We didn't have any trees then, unless you want to count the one we decorated at Christmas. Real trees, the wild kind, weren't invented until much later in my boyhood. So for my friends and me, those piles of snow were as tall as we'd get for a while: palaces and pyramids, fortresses and mountains from which, on a good day, we could see forever. For what seemed an eternity we'd climb and fall, get up and climb and fall again.

I didn't honk at anyone this morning. I drove, but I didn't honk. I kept remembering what Mr. Quinlan had said about an old fashioned winter, and I quietly thanked whoever was responsible for one more chance to climb a mountain.

*Chopping Onions*

# Roughing It At Sunset Lake

*"True Happiness ...*
*Arises From The Enjoyment Of One's Self And ...*
*From The Friendship And Conversation*
*Of A Few Select Companions."*

...Addison

Tucked in a valley between the Golden Grove and the French Village Roads is the little lake we used to call Sunset. I say "used to" not because its name has changed or anything but because I haven't been back since high school.

To get there we had to bicycle or, more than often, walk up the Grove Road to just short of where the Airport Arterial crosses it today. From there, a narrow path led through the woods for the fifteen minute hike to the southeastern shore

line. It wasn't a very big lake but it was far enough removed from the beaten track to keep it quite private. Dozens of Sunday drivers might stop at Dolan's or Shaw's on a hot summer afternoon but at Sunset we had the place all to ourselves.

The shore where we did our swimming was a sandy slope of ten or fifteen yards that led to the perfect lake bottom for wading. Farther out it got a little mucky, just before the slight drop off into deeper shadow. A fairly big rock marked the end of the gravel and beginning of the silt, and it was there that the real swimming could begin. Whenever we got tired we'd just climb up the sandy slope to a mossy area at the top where we'd sit and talk. This was important because those were the years when all of us, guys and girls alike, were working hard at unraveling the mysteries of the opposite sex, so a chance to chat casually with one's most recent infatuation was a giggly pleasure no matter what topic surfaced.

The lake itself was more or less the shape of a crescent. Its far side was grown in pretty good, except for the western end where a logging road led through the hardwood to the old Saint Patrick's Mission above Dolan's Lake. On the swim side though, a path led along the shoreline from the swimming-hole to a long-deserted cabin set in a beautiful but overgrown pine grove. When rain threatened we'd all head for the cabin where we could stay dry until the nastiness had abated.

The place had no doors or windows. As near as I can remember, it was a small, one room shack that in its time had served a basic function as a shelter and little more. I have no idea when or why it had originally become deserted but by the time we got around to using it, it was was pretty dilapidated. Still, you could tell it must have been a beautiful spot in its youth, facing directly into the setting sun over a part of the lake that was pretty well sheltered from the wind and always glassy-smooth.

Sometimes we brought our flashlights with us and stayed until after dark. That lent an air of adventure to the walk back to the road, with an added bonus of seeing the sun set before we left. On those occasions we'd stick pretty close together. After all, you never know what kind of wild animal you're going to meet in an untamed wilderness like Golden Grove: bears, and wildcats, and more bears... that kind of stuff. I guess we weren't as brave as we were adventurous.

It was on the shore of Sunset that Jim Hope and Joe Kane convinced me I should have my first overnight in the woods. I wasn't really high on the idea but the way they described it sounded so festive I decided to give it a shot. That evening the three of us packed up sleeping bags, a Coleman stove, a can of beans, a dozen rolls and a package of hotdogs and lugged the whole mess to the mossy brow at the edge of the swimming spot. By the time it started to get shadowy we had a campsite the starchiest girl guides would envy, and when it really started to get murky we lit a small fire and stick-cooked some wieners. I had to admit, this was pretty good after all.

When finally we crawled into our sleeping bags the fire was still burning quite nicely, its fifteen foot circle of light holding the darkness at a safe distance. A few pointless jokes later my lids were getting pretty heavy. Joe was the first to nod off. This didn't come as much of a surprise to Jim or me because Joe could sleep anywhere, anytime. He was even known to have dozed off riding his bike. Jim was next. He fought it for a while but finally surrendered and was gone.

It wasn't too long after that when I began to realize I wasn't all that tired after all. Worse than that, the eyelids that a little while ago were so heavy were now refusing to budge. I was cursed to lie there and stare at the darkness as the fire slowly but perceptibly died down and the inky margin crept menacingly closer. My fruitful imagination had me almost convinced I could see the outlines of tall, hairy, hungry creatures in every shadow, waiting patiently for me to nod off.

"Joe?"

No answer.

"Jim?"

Still no answer. The woods were rampant with heavy breathing.

"JIM!!!"

Jim sat up like someone who'd been skewered with a hot poker. I knew I had to think quick. That's when I felt the first drop of rain. Someone up there was taking care of me.

"Jim, I think it's starting to rain. We'll get soaked. Suppose we should wake Joe and head for the cabin?"

Mercifully, both Jim and Joe agreed. In the woods behind me I could hear the muffled sighs of disgusted creatures heading home for the night.

I must have slept through some of it though. By the time we'd gathered our provisions and started along the path to the cabin it was starting to get a little brighter. We made it just in time. Right after that, the skies opened and the torrent started.

Safe and dry inside, we decided to look bad luck in the eye and have a nice breakfast anyway. Faster than you could spit we'd unpacked the Coleman and set it up. Jim had brought along a deck of cards so we had a hand or two of crazy eights while it was heating. That's about the time we discovered our next problem: there were no wieners left. Joe, the outdoorsman of the three, was a step ahead of us. He'd had the foresight to bring along a can of beans, a BIG can of beans, just in case. Unfortunately, however, he'd neglected to bring along a pot to cook them in.

"Not a problem", Jim volunteered. "All we have to do is cook 'em right in the can. Then we can take turns spooning them out."

Sounded good to Joe and me, so we gingerly balanced the beans, container and all, on the Coleman grate and went back to our card game.

When I was in grade school I'd served my obligatory four or five years as a Cub Scout. Every year I'd received a badge for perfect attendance, but there must have been at least one meeting when I wasn't paying very close attention: the one where they tell you that cooking beans while they're still in the tin is no problem, just so long as you puncture the tin first.

I was just about to slap down my eight and declare myself the winner when the walls of the can capitulated. It wasn't like your normal, everyday-variety explosion, though. Really it was more of an intensely loud "THUNK!!" I remember seeing the first bean before I heard the noise. It flew by my ear like gigantic Junebug, only much faster, and splattered wetly against the wall to my right. It was followed by a pestilence that would have put a locust plague to shame.

Nothing was spared. Not the walls, nor the floor, nor the ceiling, nor the three of us. I have no idea how many beans are in the average can, but I can tell you this much: when liberally applied to drab walls, they leave a pleasantly beige shading, marvelously appropriate for most rural decors.

As for Joe, Jim and me, we tried our best to rinse our clothes clean before we started the walk out but we didn't have much luck. Heading down the road that morning, we must have looked like three latrine cleaners out for a stroll.

My thirst for camping wasn't nearly as strong after that outing. Give me a cozy motel room any day: one with a kitchenette, a shower and a really good can opener.

*Chopping Onions*

# Mr. Tamiaki

After nearly a week of competition here at Sydney 2000, I confess to being astounded at how smoothly everything is moving.

Take my sport, basketball, for example. Three times a day, in sessions of two games each, 10,200 fans make their way to The Dome at Olympic Park. Even allowing for the fair number who might have tickets for all the sessions, it would be reasonable to estimate fifteen to twenty thousand adventurous souls grabbing trains, busses or shuttles every day, and that's just for basketball! What about the fans of all the other sports, not to mention the just plain curious who want little more than to say they've been here.

On a couple of occasions I've taken a private shuttle reserved for technical officials but my conveyance of choice has been the train. Not only does it afford a short walk to Sydney Central, the hub of the network, but there's also some very

pleasant scenery and lots of interesting people to share one of the eighteen cars with me.

The trip itself consists of a four minute run from Town Square, just down the street from my hotel, to Central itself. Then there's a change of trains and another twenty-five minutes through the northern suburbs to the new station in Olympic Park.

It's not always the train. Sometimes I haven't a choice in the matter, like on those days when I'm stuck in The Dome until almost midnight. Then it's shuttle time, crowded tightly into a nine-person bus like sardines in a can. It's not all bad news, though. That's how I came to meet Mr. Tamiaki, a tiny little man with the widest of smiles and a personality to match. Though I'd been introduced to him earlier in the day at the hotel restaurant where he was having breakfast with his wife, there had been little if any conversation: just a brief introduction from a mutual friend and that was that.

"There goes a fascinating man", my friend Yeoh from Malaysia observed when Mr. Tamiaki had moved on. "If you get the chance, spend a few minutes with him".

That evening, fortune shone on me. Onto the shuttle climbed Mr. Tamiaki, smartly dressed in dark suit and tie and wearing a smile the width of a basketball court. Amazingly enough he recognized me immediately from our breakfast hour introduction and took the empty seat beside me.

For the next hour and a half, we talked.

Fumiya Tamiaki, it turns out, is the President and Chief Executive Officer of Molton, the maker of the official basketball of the 27th Olympiad. His leadership philosophy is a very simple one: one boss responsible for everything. He has a number of factories around the world, including in the United States, and spends one-third of the year travelling to each of them (arriving when he's least expected). A second third of his time is at his home in Hiroshima and the remainder at another home in Tokyo. His English is impeccable and his gracious friendliness most disarming.

140

He spoke of Canada and his admiration for Canadian friends, of his pride in modern Japan and of his love of basketball, a game to which I would later find he contributes significantly every year. His knowledge of Canadian geography was extensive, especially Western Canada and British Columbia. When I told him I was from Saint John, he worked his way east from Montreal and the St. Lawrence and down to Nova Scotia before the Bay of Fundy struck a familiar chord with him. Then he was okay.

He talked of the games in Australia, a country he frequently visits, and other such harmless ramblings, but what he didn't allude to was what I most wanted to hear: his boyhood and growing up in Hiroshima, and what personal memories he had of that horrific day over a half-century ago that was to change the world forever. Before I could get up the courage to ask, we were at the door of the hotel and the chance was lost. Mr. Tamiaki shook my hand once again and was gone.

I've always been a student of history, but not the history that's a blind sequence of dates and places. My love is for the characters of history, the totally human and therefore fragile parade of souls whom history genuinely touched. It's there and only there where truly worthwhile lessons are to be learned. Without them, history is little more than a timeline on a chart or scratchings on a wall.

It strikes me that Mr. Tamiaki is such a person and that I'd missed a wonderful opportunity when we parted that evening.

Time's fabric is intricately woven indeed. The stitches that give it shape are often hidden behind the colour and commotion at its surface. The 27th Olympiad is still relatively young but I've already made myself a promise: sometime before these games end, I hope to share a breakfast with Mr. Tamiaki.

*Chopping Onions*

# *Thoughts On The Conclusion Of The Sydney Olympic Games*

When I was fifteen or sixteen, I went to a movie called "On The Beach". It was the beginning of the cold war and much of the sensible world was unnerved with the prospect of a nuclear holocaust. The movie exploited that premise, with its final scenes set in Australia as what was left of humankind awaited the radioactive cloud that would end it all.

The theme music for the movie was Waltzing Matilda. I had no idea what the words meant but nonetheless was captivated by the hauntingly sad yet defiant melody. Long after the movie had ended, the song remained with me and for forty

143

years I've hummed it without understanding it, like admiring the Mona Lisa without a thought for the smile.

That's no longer the case. The games of the 27th Olympiad both opened and closed with the sweet strains of Matilda and have affected me in ways deeper and more personal than I might ever have expected.

Understand this isn't something unique to me alone. I've seen it, especially in these last few days, in athletes, coaches, volunteers: anyone associated at all with what has happened over the two week period that was the games. For some it was manifested in the need for a quiet moment alone; for others, it might have been hugs or tears, high-fives or back slaps, a nervous laugh or the inexplicable urge to scream as loud as one can scream.

The commonality was that the moment was always accompanied with flashes of introspection, for me reaching far deeper than ever I've been within the soul that defines me.

When I arrived here in Australia, it was with mixed emotions. On the up side, this would be (as my wife urged me) a once-in-a-lifetime opportunity: "When are you likely to have another chance to go to Australia!" There was no denying that one! Then there was the anticipation of working with old friends from other countries, making some new ones and the reality of courtside seats for some great basketball.

On the down side, I was committed to two weeks of work around Oz after the completion of competition, and the thought of being away from home for five weeks was more than a little distressing.

My reservations were correct. Each day was longer than the day before. If I stayed busy, the time went quickly, but the hour or two before bedding down was interminable. I missed Tim Horton's and the Nature Park and driving my children to school and university; Friday afternoon at the Barrack Green and having a coffee at noon with Barb. I'm a big boy now and I survived, but not without a few emotional bursts of the "I wanna go home" variety more befitting a kid's first day at school.

So what did I learn from my experience? Three things come to mind.

First, I'm so damn proud of being Canadian. Everyone I've met, every single person, has praised the image of Canada and Canadians. We are seen by the world as friendly and fair, two qualities of immeasurable value in the global community. Sure, I got lots of queries about whether or not I knew so-and-so in Calgary, Toronto or Montreal, and lots of people had no idea there was a Canada east of Quebec, but that ignorance is of geography, not Canadians.

Second, I continue to be amazed at the human ability to rise from apparent ashes. Again and again at these games I watched as athletes reached deep inside and tapped whatever source necessary to do what must be done. In many cases the effort could only be termed heroic and left them at the point of exhaustion; yet each of them is a human being, as human and vulnerable as you and I. The same ability is reflected in news-reel faces from East Timor, Ethiopia, Yugoslavia and Columbia. There's a lesson to be learned for those of us so fortunate as never to have been tested.

Finally and most of all, I've been blessed to learn something many others have paid dearly to realize: the irreplaceable, immeasurable value of family. I now fully understand how important each of them is to me. Ironically, I'd always assumed I already knew this but it took a separation of these many weeks and many thousands of miles for the truth to catch fire.

No doubt I'll have other travelling to do in the future but never again for so long: that I promise. Time is too precious. And though I may go away, I'll never leave. In my heart I'll take them with me.

*Chopping Onions*

# *On Trees*

### *"Keep A Green Tree In Your Heart*
### *And Perhaps The Singing Bird Will Come."*

...Chinese Proverb

The enormous pine sat at the top of a gentle slope just beyond the narrow brook. To reach it we had to park the car on the Broad Road, precisely four miles on the Fredericton side of Petersville Hill. An old logging road at times little more than a path led us on a fifteen or twenty minute meander from the highway to the stream's edge, disappeared in the shallow water, and resurfaced briefly on the other side. By the time it reached our pine, there wasn't much left to it. From here on, we were on our own.

The tree itself was gigantic. Its base was probably fifteen feet in circumference, and the ground immediately below was relatively clear of undergrowth. Magnificent branches sheltered the earth from the rain, leaving it relatively dry, the perfect place to set up our Coleman stove for noon meal.

By the time we dropped by each October, the sweet odour of autumn was everywhere and the brook had overcome its August trickle to bubble and froth excitedly. Behind the tree spread a forest that stretched all the way to Blissville. To the south, the nearest settlement to speak of was Welsford; to the north, Garey; and to the east, Route 7. Then nothing until the Saint John River a million miles away. A few hundred yards downstream sat a venerable old beaver dam, its heavy mud banks well flattened by years of deer and moose traffic and the occasional Gagetown soldier. Other than that the place was ours.

Originally it belonged to Joe Breen. I say "belonged" in

the spiritual sense because access to the land itself was Camp Gagetown's responsibility. Nevertheless Joe had spent a goodly part of his youth there and knew it intimately. In the late `60's, after Terry Comeau and I joined the staff at Saint Malachy's, Joe took pity on us and decided to show us some "real huntin' country". Hugh Whalen, our principal at the time, found us equally pathetic and introduced us to Mount Pisca, near Sussex, but it was Joe's country where we spent most of our time.

We weren't great hunters, Terry and I. I guess maybe we secretly empathized with the deer. Bill Coffey took pernicious delight in describing how the squirrels would anticipate our arrival and gather at the edge of the road to meet us. Then they'd run up and down our gun barrels chattering excitedly while rabbits rubbed warmly against our ankles. He loved to conjure the image of Terry and I bearing a pith-helmeted Joe on our shoulders, binoculars hanging from his neck, while an animal choir chortled the Alleluia Chorus in the distance.

Usually we'd head into the woods while it was still dark. That way we'd reach the tree about the time it was starting to brighten a little, deposit our cooking paraphernalia in the alders on the other side of the brook and venture forth for the morning's hunt. We could always count on starting a partridge or two before sunrise, but even when we didn't the walk was well worth the effort. We'd go our separate ways and meet again around noon back at the tree. Then we'd fire up the Coleman, throw on a few steaks, and have a banquet like you wouldn't believe.

There's something about a meal in the woods that the best of restaurants couldn't hope to emulate, especially on a chilly autumn afternoon, legs stiff from a few hours walking. I think the odours are the best part: potatoes first, then tons of onions, then the meat, and finally a can or two of mushrooms. While we waited, a steaming mug of coffee cupped in both hands helped us forget the musky dampness of the ground. On more than one occasion we might even snooze for a few minutes.

Over the years these meals became a tradition. The last day of the hunt was reserved for a special feast with all the trimmings we could muster. I'd load the back seat with a folding metal table of my father's that could be carried like a fair-sized suitcase. Inside it were four small chairs to complete the ensemble. At meal time on the last day we'd trek back out to the highway, deposit our rifles in the trunk, and head in again with our table, a cooler full of goodies, and a sip of wine. Then, in the shade of the Petersville woods, we'd set a table worthy of "Better Homes And Gardens". There'd be real cutlery (none of that cheap plastic stuff), an honest to goodness tablecloth, plates and cups, even wine glasses. When everything was ready we'd pull up a chair (three chairs really) and chow down. The only thing missing was the tuxedos.

I remember the afternoon we were half way through our meal when another hunter happened by. Try to imagine the scenario. The poor guy probably had been doing some heavy tracking since dawn and had likely reached the point where he was convinced he and his deer had the entire forest to themselves. Nose to the earth, ear to the slightest shuffle, he'd been plodding faithfully for lord knows how long until he reached the evergreen grove behind our pine. Then, head down, hand on the brim of his hat, he'd pushed his way through the broad branches to find... to find three guys sitting at a table eating steaks and sipping wine!

Joe spoke first. "Morning."

No reply. Just a blank stare, like one might wear after blundering into the wrong washroom.

"Lovely morning. See any signs?" Joe was being especially neighbourly this morning.

Terry lipped his wine glass and returned to his T-bone.

Our visitor shook his head slightly, entirely confused by the incongruity into which he'd wandered.

"Cookie?", Joe offered as the stranger began to back away.

"No. Thank you. But... Well, I've gotta..." He pointed in the general direction of the spruce stand from which he'd emerged only a moment before, mumbled something about its getting late and then left as quickly as he'd arrived. Quicker probably.

For many years we returned faithfully each October to our tree by the brook. It always seemed as happy to see us as we were to be back. No, it never said as much, but when you spend a lot of time with trees you get to feel what they're thinking. And trees may be very poor speakers, but they listen better than most humans I know. An old Vancouver friend, `Wink' Willox (his real name was John but he preferred Wink) taught me this, and whenever I think of that old pine I also remember Wink because they both faded away about the same time.

Wink was someone whom I first met at a basketball meeting in the early 1970's. He was a gray-haired old gentleman who was a legend in his sport. Fittingly, he was posthumously elected to the Canadian Basketball Hall of Fame a few years ago, thirteen years after his passing.

Anyway, Wink had a pretty tough time the last few months of his life. Usually he'd be most uncomfortable late in the evening, just before bedtime. That's when he'd pick up the phone and give me a call; "just to jaw a bit", he'd say. The trouble was, ten or eleven o'clock in the evening is two or three a.m. Saint John time! Whenever the phone would ring in the wee hours of the morning, my wife Barb would observe "Let's hope it's Wink!"

For whatever reason, he always seemed to feel better after a half hour's talk and that's what really mattered. For my part, I learned more about life (and death) in those ten or fifteen phone calls than I had in four years of university classes.

He last call was a few nights before he died. It was the best I'd heard him sound in a long while.

"You're chipper tonight, Wink. Something special going on?"

I could hear a slight chuckle on the other end.

"No, not out of the ordinary anyway. I just had a really good visit with my tree today. That always helps."

He'd caught me off guard.

"Your tree?"

"Well, it's not my tree. Just one I've adopted for a while."

"Speak to me, Wink."

"It's down in Stanley Park, on a little path just off one of the main walkways. It's huge, a real giant. Whenever I feel up to it I go over there and we talk."

"You what?"

"I talk to it!"

"You really talk to it; like `hello', `how are you', `good-bye', ...stuff like that?"

His tone was more serious now. Almost meditative.

"I guess it really doesn't matter that it's a tree. Just so long as it's alive and been around a lot longer than you have. And you don't have to talk out loud either. Just like, you know, talking in your head. All I know is I always feel better afterwards."

The big pine that Joe, Terry and I used to visit is gone now. The brook's gone too, at least gone in the physical sense. But whenever I pass the spot where we'd park the car on those cold October mornings, I can imagine it rising through the mists, patiently waiting for three guys and a table.

It's too bad Joe and Terry didn't get to meet Wink. I think they'd have liked each other.

# *Ben Lomond*

Stand on the site where Centracare used to be. Now look to the east, over the top of the city and toward the airport. What appear to be three adjacent mountains stand on the horizon like a triple-humped camel. See them? If you were to look side-on, you'd be able to appreciate they're really two, not three, but why quibble. From this vantage point it's also difficult to comprehend their size or the sharp angle of their slope but the larger of the bunch clearly forms the highest point of land for many miles around.

The smaller doesn't have a formal name that I've heard, though I'm sure there is one. My father, who was born on the farmland that lies at its westerly base, always called it "the high hill". The larger of the two, the one that edges on the Loch Lomond Lakes, is Ben Lomond Mountain.

Until the construction of the airport arterial a decade or more ago, this wooded retreat was essentially untouched, frequented only by locals and, in season, the occasional hunter or fisherman. For me personally, it was a place built for recreation, the perfect setting to sit or wander as the spirit moved me.

In warmer months we'd fish. My favourite spot was on the northern incline, a small, boomerang-shaped lake hidden at the end of a double-rutted road. Once there was a camp here too, complete with boathouse and children's swings, but it burned one winter and all that's left is a scar. The lake really wasn't a "lake" but more the illusion of a lake. In reality, it was just a very wide brook that fed first into one pond and then into another. To us though, it was a private fishing hole, isolated from the beaten track. It's still there if you've a mind to go for a leisurely walk but you'll have to find it for yourself.

Sometimes we'd take another logging road off what is now the Cosy Lake Road. You had to be pay close attention or you'd miss the entrance but it was just beyond where the Driscoll family (remember Driscoll's Drugs on Union?) had a summer camp. It ran a wide semi-circle around Ben Lomond Mountain to come out on the Loch Lomond Lake at a spot called Sandy Shore. Here one might hook onto a land-locked salmon or a more than decent lake trout, either one a trophy well worth the walk.

Even without a fish, the late afternoon experience made it worth the effort. After the first fifty yards, the road yielded to a narrow path that meandered through alternating stands of hardwood and softwood as it wound around the skirt of the mountain. If you could be quiet long enough to listen, a natural symphony would entertain you: bird songs, squirrel chatter, the whispering of leaves. On really special late evenings there might even be a deer along the way.

Ben Lomond Mountain was a climb and a half. One or two spots were quite sheer and had to be circled but most of the slope was manageable if you took your time. The most difficult approach was from the north. Enormous boulders and scores of moss-covered logs and fallen trees lay chaotically, making every step a climb in itself. Near the top, an ancient, yawning crevice about a foot wide, the product of the same upheaval that created the lakes below, split much of the mountain crest into two pieces.

The view from the top was as spectacular then as it is today: the big lakes to the east, airport to the south, the city to the west and the hills of the Kingston Peninsula to the north. Somewhere here there is a plaque, my father once told me. It was erected by some government body long ago to acknowledge the altitude and has since been covered by the flotsam and jetsam of aging woodland. Here also is a grassy plateau pocked with the flattened bowls of grass that mark where deer have lain for centuries of summer evenings, a perfect stop for a sandwich and thermos of coffee after a long climb.

Alas, progress can be disheartening sometimes. A paved highway now climbs through one of the mountain notches and then downhill to the airport on the other side. The second notch has fallen victim to the lumberman's saw and a few years ago was stripped clean of any appreciable growth. But the mountains are still there, and new growth is already reclaiming what was laid bare.

Few people visit the Ben Lomond anymore, which ironically provides an answer to that old question about a tree falling in the forest. Each evening, despite the absence of an audience, nature's symphony continues to perform.

*Chopping Onions*

# *Old Photographs And Me*

When my brother and I were growing up, there always were lots of photographs around the house. Besides the framed ones that hung from the walls or decorated bureaus and tables, there were five or six old albums tucked away in an enormous dresser that my father had built and which occupied one corner of my parents' room.

It was easy to tell by the wear of the front covers which albums contained the oldest pictures. Some went back as far as 1915 or 1916 when my father was just a little sprout; those of my mother's family dated back to the 1930's, in the years before she and my father married. Then there was the inevitable assortment of growing-up photos of my brother and me,

resplendent with Teddy Bears, tricycles and Christmas trees.

I remember how much I enjoyed thumbing through each one when I got the chance, bugging my mother for a name now and then so as to put a label to the faces. I was especially intrigued with the people I hadn't had the chance to meet but whom I'd heard my parents mention on occasions when we had visitors: great-grandparents, distant uncles, aunts and cousins who had died before my time.

I guess it was inevitable that my fascination with photo-watching would eventually evolve into photo-taking. My parents must have sensed this on the Christmas they gave me my first camera, a little plastic Kodak Brownie with a flash attachment that could be mounted to the side when needed. With it came a tan vinyl carrying case, a couple of films, a dozen flash bulbs and a plastic shield to put over the flash just in case the bulb burst when it went off.

In the next week and a half, I must have taken a hundred pictures. I was lucky because a family friend who was also a distant cousin worked at a photo studio uptown and got me all my film for nothing. Not only that but she'd also develop my pictures and print them without charge, although the final prints were especially small.

I started with scenes around the house and along my street, and then moved on to the surrounding neighbourhood. On weekends, my friend John Walsh and I would go for walks around Fisher Lakes (they were the "Arches" to us, a derivative from "artificial" or man-made), taking pictures of whatever moved and much that didn't. My favourite spot was the makeshift zoo with the bears in their concrete enclosures. I'd watch and wait, sometimes for an hour at a time, until they'd do something I considered photogenic, like scratch their backs against the wall. They weren't always cooperative, though; more than often I'm come away with a shot of what looked like a discarded carpet on a concrete floor.

As I grew older and my photo collection continued to

expand, I got lazy. Taking the time to arrange photos neatly in albums, like my parents had done, became less entertaining than the picture-taking itself. Shoeboxes were the answer. Each could hold hundreds of pictures and then be stored away in a minimum of space. When I later got married and the number of photos in my collection doubled and tripled, my wife Barb was always after me to get them organized. But what did I do? I choose the easy way out and took up colour slides in carousels. For a while this worked well but then I got lazy again and even stopped labeling the carousels any more than I had to. Finally I'd gone full circle and was back once more to colour prints and shoe boxes.

For almost ten years after my mother's death, my father took loving care of his albums. When he too died in the 1996, I brought them home to stay with me, but when I looked through them this time there was a difference. What I had inherited was more than a collection of fading photographs; I'd also come into the responsibility of preserving the memories they embodied, memories that by now included me.

I take better care of my pictures now. I finally understand the inestimable contribution family albums like these make to our appreciation of who we were, where we are and what we might become. In a world riddled with unknowns, the consoling security that a family album can afford is limited only by one's reluctance to remember.

*Chopping Onions*

# *Benny Goldstein*

I've always been somewhat of a music nut, though admittedly there have been highs and lows in my devotion. Like most of us, however, a safe guess would be my high school and university years were my most melodically passionate.

I think it started the night Elvis was on the Dorsey Brother's variety show. Before then, I'd been content just to listen to the radio, but after that historic appearance I stepped it up a notch. Following a decent amount of cajoling, my parents bought me a record player and I was off to the musical races.

The machine was pretty standard for its day; a squarish box, portable, light brown or gray, with a hinged lid that lifted to reveal a rudimentary turntable slightly smaller than the records it accepted. Immediately surrounding the sprocket was a circular bit of plastic that could be raised to accommodate the larger center holes that characterized 45 rpm's.

Along with it came my very first 78, Elvis's "Don't Be Cruel"; they didn't come any cooler than that! For the next few weeks it was the only record I had, so it got a good workout, good enough to convince my parents to get me another recording as quickly as possible. Pretty soon everyone in our extended family knew what to get Freddy for Christmas, birthday, or whatever; my collection grew exponentially.

By the time my brother Jim got around to collecting, the market had moved from 78's to 45's and we bought a bunch of those small storage cases, with the wood-grain paper on the sides, to hold them all. Handy little alphabetized index dividers came with them but they usually were lost within the week. After all, half the fun was searching through the whole bunch to find the platter you wanted.

Saturday was our musical shopping day and there was only one place to go: Ben Goldstein's store on Union Street, just around the corner from Waterloo. To my friends and myself, it was a gathering spot that ranked right up there with the Louie Green's at the head of King or the Charlotte Street entrance to Woolworth's. One wall was lined with a number of listening areas, much like telephone booths, where we could review a potential purchase before laying out our $1.25. The proprietor, Ben himself ("Mr. Goldstein" to us in those days), was a tiny man with wavy black hair and black-rimmed glasses who knew every recording in his inventory and who could find in twenty seconds whatever it was you were looking for. I can still see him shuffling along like a man on a mission, moving much faster than his short legs should have allowed.

He must have been a person with as much patience as entrepreneurial know-how because he always treated us with trust, so long as we respected him in the same way. We were only too aware of the consequence of violating our symbiotic relationship: the welcome mat would be unceremoniously removed. I have no idea if Ben ever had to execute his implicit threat but I can truthfully say I never heard any of my friends speak ill of him.

By the time I was in university, Ben had moved his shop next door to the Riviera Restaurant. Whenever I'd return from university for a weekend or an extended holiday, I'd drop by to say hello and to check out his stock. The only music store in Antigonish was dreadfully understocked and by that time I was getting heavily into folk music. Ben's hair was a little lighter but that was the only modification. He still could scurry with the best of them and knew every album (by then I was into 33 1/3's) on the market. What he didn't have, he would order, but there was precious little he didn't have.

After I returned to Saint John for good and began teach-ing, my reliance on Goldstein's "for all my music needs" (a promise he never forgot) didn't end. I bought my first console stereo through him, and two guitars and a banjo. Until his store finally closed for good, I saw him almost every business day after school, and I guarantee I bought a ton of records.

It wasn't until he did close down, however, that I realized something. Over the years, my years, without my being conscious of the growth, he'd gone from "Mr. Goldstein" to "Ben" to "Benny".

The trust and indeed the seeds of friendship sown when I was a teenager had taken root.

The music had become secondary.

*Chopping Onions*

# *New Year's*

I have a confession to make. I know; it'll probably leave anyone under the age of twenty howling indignation but I've got to "'fess up" anyway: in the hierarchy of things I look forward to, the six days before New Year's is more important to me than the six weeks before Christmas. Not in the spiritual sense, mind you; Midnight Mass is still the most meaningful hour of my year, and the serenity of a manger scene rejuvenates a part of me which I'm ashamed to admit may lie dormant forty-eight weeks out of fifty-two. No, it's earthier than that, more temporal. The way I figure it, it's got a lot to do with age.

Christmas, at least the secular part characterized by ribbons and wrapping, is indeed for children. At their age they can be forgiven for not zealously picking up on the religious dimension of the season. After all, they're just following our lead. For weeks and sometimes months they're assailed with images the very antithesis of the simple manger message. "What do you want from Santa?", we impishly grill. "Have you been good all year"? And what is the proffered reward for not crying or pouting? The promise of more loot than you can shake a stick at, that's what. So children, innately very good at following the lead, expect in kind. Sadly, Christmas is demoted to a season of getting rather than giving, and love is measured in the degree of gratification secured.

And where are we adults through all of this? From early November through Christmas Eve we pay the price, both literally and figuratively. "Shop 'till you drop" becomes the catch phrase as we scour the malls for those bargains that make the season "gayer". Sure, part of it's fun, like hiding the booty and trimming the tree, but for the most part it's an exhausting exercise that exacts a toll both physical and psychological. Come

Christmas Day, any satisfaction inherent in watching the kids dive in is directly proportional to whatever degree of difficulty there may be in keeping our eyes open. Lost in the chaos are the peace, generosity and sharing intrinsic to the true message of the season: love. Not a love that is conditional, but complete and absolute, freely offered and humbly received. Older children begin to catch on when they take the important step of choosing for themselves the gifts that they will give to the ones they love. Only then does Christmas become a "giving" exercise, the joy of the moment inseparable from the expressions on the faces of those who receive. Then and only then does the "giving" and "getting" merge as sharing.

That's where December 27 to January 1 has the edge. At sunrise on Boxing Day you can almost hear the door slam on yet another Christmas. No more jingle bells and Bing Crosby, Scrooge and Canadian Tire, or Anne Murray sing-alongs. Abandoned Christmas trees gather at the side of the road, waiting for the finality of the shredder as winter takes hold in earnest. With the pressure off and the new year approaching, it=s a time for stock-taking of a different kind, a time to review the profoundly simple things that we tend to lose sight of in the confusion of today's overtly materialistic Christmas season. The older we become, the more immediate the implications of a passing year, and the reality can be very sobering. It is a time for cultivating those bonds of kin and friendship that we can sometimes take for granted in the brightness of a July sun. A game with our children, the sharing of a dusty photograph album, an embrace with no motive but the embrace itself. These are the signs of the season, and the culmination of it all is New Year's Eve. Unlike the bedlam of Christmas preparations, we kind of slide into New Year's, the pact set by no more than setting suns and the growing awareness that days are slowly but surely getting longer.

This New Year's like last will be spent with a friends. Yes, there'll be food and ample bubbly, but what's more important will be the conversation and sharing: old anecdotes drawn from time's footlocker, favourite jokes reviewed just one more time, governments assailed and the departed praised, all in the interest of closure. We gently remind each other that most of us qualify for the Seniors discount at Tim Horton's, while enthusiastically insisting today's music doesn't hold a candle to what we grew up with, and outside the living room where we sit the world is falling apart. Then at the appropriate moment we toast the hour, hug, shake hands, slap backs, have a good yawn and head home for another year, both touched and renewed by the warmth of lifelong friendships.

# Apologia

It strikes me odd
that one man's recollection is,
quite possibly,
another's prevarication.

I mean, if I say to you
"Do you remember ...",
and you say to me
"Sure I do!",
you might have no idea
what it is I'm talking about,
or your recall be entirely different from mine
but you're too embarrassed to correct me.

*Chopping Onions*

Perhaps I'm overly concerned
and it's nothing to worry about,
but the fact that
the best of my memories involve others
leaves me a little apprehensive.

Do they remember as I?

Do they remember at all?

Is what I remember
the way it really was?

Or have I,
in some grotesque metaphysical reversal,
reframed experience,
re-ordered reality.

I have no doubt that
such speculation
in moments of anguished solitude
has driven more than one Platonist
off the deep end.

But not me.
I've learned to adapt:
no longer preface recollection
with apology,
am content to tell it
the way it is,
see memory, like all realities
imagined or otherwise,
'the stuff that dreams are made of'.